Lighten Up to Be Enlightened!

– The 50 Rules of Joy

By J.M. Davies

Virtuous Arts

www.virtuousarts.com

http://bit.ly/VirtuousArts

Published by Virtuous Arts 2015

Copyright © 2015 J.M. Davies
All Rights Reserved.

ISBN 978-952-68383-0-4

FOR MY DAUGHTER COCO

— Thanks to you I have been able to increase my awareness through and for love.

"A graceful flow of beauty and elegance, 'Lighten Up To Be Enlightened!' is delightful. Formulated with love and enlightenment, J.M. Davies guides you on your spiritual journey to a blissful, loving existence."

– Dr. Michael C. Hudak,
D.C., NLP Master Practitioner, drhudak.com

"Happiness is ours to claim – many of us make it too complicated. In this book J.M. Davies gives us simple tools to reclaim our joy and love our lives."

– Janice Madariaga, Speaker/Author/Coach

"With this book, you want to savour every word written, but at the same time rush to the next page to see what wonderful lies ahead. This is the kind of book, that by the time you finish, you want to start all over again."

– Pirita Valtonen, Fundraising Planner and a mother

CONTENTS

Acknowledgements

Thank you for everyone who has influenced the birth of my first self-help book. Thank You for those people who have inspired me to love them. Thank you for having let me love you. Thank you Coco who has inspired me to write this book so that anyone who reads these words could benefit from the mistakes I have made and from which I have learnt to enjoy the joy of living – even when I make so-called mistakes. Learning to surrender to life and accept the present moment with a light heart helps you to live your life to the fullest. I hope this book will encourage you to make your own mistakes and when you look back you can see them as a blessing that you needed at that particular time in your life.

Thank you all the proofreaders like Mikko, Jarmo and Mirva for your insightful comments and the technical people like Ari for your help. Thanks to all my spiritual teachers and people who have inspired me on this path, like Pepe and Bob. Thank You, dear reader, for taking time to read this book. I hope it will inspire you to take the required action needed to live the life of your dreams. I hope you will find the peace, love and joy inside yourself that makes this life blissful and you'll connect yourself with others so that your light can be spread around you.

Introduction

When I was telling about this book to a friend of mine, he asked me why do I want to experience enlightenment. I considered it a funny question because I couldn't think of any reason why wouldn't someone like to be enlightened. For me enlightenment is synonymous with the fullest life possible. And who wouldn't want to experience life to the fullest? Of course there are many other definitions for enlightenment. To Andy Shaw it means to be oneself, whereas the Merriam-Webster dictionary defines it as:

The state of having knowledge or understanding: the act of giving someone knowledge or understanding

Buddhism: a final spiritual state marked by the absence of desire or suffering.

I was born into a Christian family in a Christian country. Meeting some narrow-mindedness in those circles led me to seek elsewhere. The Christian education I received was in many ways helpful in order to live a good life, like was reading Aristotle. However, it had been the light of God that had always intrigued me because I felt that the Truth exists already, we just need to shed some light to reveal it. When I became a yoga teacher and I was given a name that meant the light of the world, wanting to become enlightened was a done deal.

However, even if *wanting* to become enlightened was pointing me towards a helpful lifestyle, it always kept me *wanting* the enlightenment. It was not until surrendered I fully, that I experienced what enlightenment could be like. One day I was on a mountaintop in Spain looking at the sea and a *Stupa,* a huge Buddhist statue used as a place of meditation, on the mountain opposite to me when I had the most beautiful experience of my life.

It felt like someone had lifted a veil that was on me. All the colours I saw were richer and I felt a total unconditional love towards all sentient beings. There was no suffering, nor a reason for suffering anymore. It was like I had woken up from a sleep. Everything I used to think was real, wasn't real but just an illusion I, and everyone around me, had believed for centuries. All I could do was smile.

That experience was short and I wanted to experience it again, so I continued to follow the ethical and physical conduct my yoga school had taught me. I became very mindful and meditated in different ways. Still I was not able to experience that beautiful experience again until I gave up and started to pursue motherhood more than enlightenment.

One day as I was having a picnic with a pregnant friend, I experienced it again as I had given up also on becoming pregnant and I was just truly happy that my friend was able to experience the Earthly experience I imagined to be the most beautiful one for any woman. Then suddenly the colours changed again and I felt like I was everyone, I was my pregnant friend and the baby inside her womb, I was the trees and the grass. It was completely euphoric.

Third time I experienced "the enlightenment" after giving dance and yoga classes, and it was the shortest of them all. Then I also saw some special lights because that was the only time I was inside and was not able to experience the real beauty of the nature surrounding us.

Then I became a mother and was able to experience the most beautiful Earthly experience so far.

As I was doing the final editing of this book, my daughter lost her consciousness due to a sudden sickness. For a moment I thought I had lost her for good. After I had called the ambulance, I was holding her in my arms in an empty square and shouted that my daughter has died. Luckily the ambulance arrived very quickly and she recovered. Now I can enjoy a bit longer this Earthly experience with her.

That incident further clarified to me that I want to lighten up to enjoy every day to the fullest and help others do the same. It also crystallized to me that life is meant to destroy our bodies and enrich our souls. And if, by grace, we are ready to receive enlightenment, it will be given to us when we let go and least expect it – like all the best things in life. May reading this book enrich your soul and make your life more enjoyable until you are fully enlightened.

"When you feel a peaceful joy, that's when you are near truth."
– Rumi

Command your subconscious mind to lighten up!

Would you like to be peacefully joyful every day of your life? Just sit back and enjoy the read – it could be the beginning of your more joyful existence.

This book is based on my self-help novel "Apsara's Dance" and the blog "Enjoying the Joy" and further developed through NLP methods and my coaching experience to lighten the load of life for you. However, ultimately it is your decision to allow it to happen or not. I'm not saying that you'll reach enlightenment by reading this book but I am saying that unless you can't recognize the emptiness of life, you can't reach enlightenment.

The concept of the book is simple and easy to follow, yet it includes powerful insights about how you can make your human existence lighter – meaning both increasing the light over darkness and lightness over heaviness in your being. Use the space at the end of this book to write down, and why not also draw, your own moments of light!

Start with faith. Just allow yourself to trust the process and begin. Command your subconscious mind to observe yourself and the world as honestly as possible with fifteen different rules. Then start to have certainty about your beliefs and command yourself to meditate with another fifteen rules. Doing this you will hear your inner guidance and will be ready to receive joy. After you have received joy, you will want to give it back. You will want to love – and experience even more joy. Then command yourself with twenty rules to act virtuously in this world, making the best use of your talents and interests.

Now I ask you to ask yourself: are you living your life to the fullest? What are you waiting for? Lighten up to be enlightened! Don't think that it would always be easy for me to follow that command. I am a highly sensitive person and tend to take things very seriously because of my natural temperament. It has its benefits but personally I have noticed that learning to let go of the heaviness of life and lightening up has the greatest potential for making my own life euphoric.

Lightening up doesn't mean that you no longer find anything sacred or that you would belittle yours or other people's effort or sorrows, it just helps you to shed the light on everything you encounter so that you can see things more clearly and make the necessary changes either in yourself or in your circumstances to live your best life. Lighten up to be enlightened also means to me that we don't take the stories of our egos so seriously even if we will listen to them and respect them and the feelings that are attached to them. Listening to the stories with a light heart helps you to discover the wisdom embedded in them.

I also wish you will read this book with a light heart so that you can make the best use of the words that my love for my daughter has poured out also for your benefit. Read it from cover to cover or open any page you'd like and you'll hear the message you will need to hear at that time. Don't be discouraged by the occasional down days, they are reminding you of the progress you have made so far and showing you new possibilities for expanding your joy. Just be open to enjoy the joy every moment of your life like it was the first and the last!

I SELF- AND WORLD-OBSERVATION (Faith)

"I used to be a perfectionist, but I'm trying to improve." – Fray Pascual

What does your faith smell like? My faith smells like freshly squeezed orange juice. What does your joy taste like? My joy tastes like the kisses of my beloved. What does your peace feel like? Mine feels like soft summer wind caressing my hair and moving my silk dress around my body. What does your love look like? Mine looks like a pink sunset. What does your hope sound like? Mine sounds like my daughter's laugh.

In addition to your mind and imagination, use your senses when observing yourself and the world. Know that you can find beauty in yourself and life.

Rule nr 1: Know your paradise!

"Ask yourself whether the dream of heaven and greatness should be waiting for us in our graves - or whether it should be ours here and now and on this earth." – Ayn Rand

The Paradise on Earth

The idea of a Heaven, Paradise, Shambhala, Utopia, Shangri-La, has always intrigued people. Have you ever wondered why?

Some psychologists say it comes from the early experiences of a baby merging with his or her mother while drinking milk from the mother's bosom and falling asleep while doing it. I believe it is something in-built in us and we get glimpses of it as we merge together with a beloved – whether in a child-mother relationship, or as two lovers, or as an ecstatic connection to God.

When I blogged about this at the age of 30, I felt grateful for having gotten everything else in life that I could have possibly asked for, except a child. I still wanted to bring peace to the whole world and stop the suffering of all the sentient beings, but with accomplishing that I had given myself time until the end of my life. Now at the age of 36, I am a proud and happy mother of a healthy daughter and only those more universal dreams remain unfulfilled, while I accidentally continue to discover beauty that I didn't even have a clue could exist.

Unfulfilled desires make me humble. There are still numerous things out of our control in this world. We just have to have faith, hope and love. These three aspects of human life make life worthwhile. While we are in this world, we need all of them, but as we enter Paradise, the only thing needed is love. I believe that living in and for love is the closest we can come to achieving Heaven on earth.

Longing for Shambhala is paradoxical; one knows that in order to attain that blissful place, one has to be able to first attain the blissful state of being. So, let's concentrate on getting you to the blissful state!

It starts from accepting yourself and life as it is but not necessarily accepting it as the unchangeable truth. So, let's put you in focus.

Sainthood for the Selfish

Be selfish for a moment and write down your wishes and dreams. Don't censor yourself, write down everything that tickles your fancy. You want to know *You,* not the you that is socially acceptable. Then put that paper away somewhere from where you can find it after a couple of months to see if any of them have come true.

In the meantime, be as grateful and virtuous as you can in every situation you encounter. Above all, however, love everybody to the best of your ability – also yourself. Think and talk kindly and see how that makes you and people around you feel. If you are not able to think kindly, you have probably neglected fulfilling your own needs or you don't know how to ask help for fulfilling them. Work on this and your life will become enchanted!

I am living my dream! I write this in the Bahamas occasionally glancing towards the white sandy beach followed by the turquoise ocean. I have eaten fresh fruit – I have never seen so big peaches before – I have practiced yoga and meditation, swam, read and written some. This is the selfish part of my dream life. The other, unselfish part, is giving back to God and the world through service. I hope that taking care of my own needs – the sunlight, time outside in the nature, rest, right kind of food and exercise, the pleasure of aesthetics and the company of like-minded people – will enable me to give back joyfully.

I pay careful attention to the things I can be grateful for and thank other people involved whenever I can in different ways: sometimes with words, sometimes with smiles, sometimes as a tip, sometimes as a helping hand or a prayer. Loving service can take many different forms. I humbly hope that my writing can be of service to some people. I believe that taking care of my hygiene and looks can be considered a service to the people around me. I intend to look and smell good for the wellbeing of everybody, not in order to boost my ego. I am convinced that my praying for the world and its inhabitants is an important service even if no one can ever prove their effect.

We are supposed to enjoy our lives in a virtuous way. Not to deny pleasures in order to get closer to God or neglect our own needs in order to fulfill other people's needs. This Earth could be a paradise for us all, we don't need to hoard or compete with others in order to find happiness. We just need to make ourselves lovable to ourselves first. When we feel lovable, we can accept the free gifts of the Universe that our Creator is giving us in different ways, often times using other people – angels in disguise – to manifest them.

Heaven Is Where the Heart Is

I'm back home in Finland now and I love it even if it is not sunny and doesn't have the tropical heat of the Bahamas. I have reconnected with many beautiful souls I missed whilst abroad. There is always something pleasant about our physical surroundings as well as something negative – if you want to look at it that way.

When I saw a book called *Utopia* in the local bookshop, it made me think that my utopia is a place where everyone is virtuous and healthy. Everybody is peacefully joyful as they perform the duties they have themselves chosen to make the best use of their talents in order to make the society well-functioning. Everybody lives in abundance. In my utopia we are able to be vulnerable at all times because of everybody's saintly nature nobody will try to manipulate or use anyone in any way. Nobody has to fear in this place

16

because nobody is needy due to the constant connection to the Divine Source of loving energy. Mercy is its religion and the politics is based on perfect justice.

How can we reach this paradise? In the end everyone wants to live in a loving world. Do your thoughts contribute to the making of this place a more loving one? Anything negative is lack of love. Because we'll get to the paradise one person at a time, we have to start looking at our minds and hearts. We – and the societal structures – should lovingly encourage people to become more and more virtuous. In order for people to stay motivated to develop their virtues, they will have to enjoy it. What has encouraged or inspired you to develop your virtues?

Finding Your Fairy Tale

What was your favorite fairy tale as a child? Does that still influence your life? Are you consciously or unconsciously trying to live that fairy tale true in your life? Is that what you really want or should you leave that childhood dream behind and create your own fairy tale?

There exists a wide discussion on what fairy tales actually are but I leave that aside now defining fairy tale here as the script on how your life would ideally unfold your personal utopia.

Happiness is the goal for most people – whether it is conscious or unconscious. The ways to happiness vary considerably according to one's personality and life experiences, culture and so forth. Then one has to find a balance between instant gratification and long-term joy. The more mature and pure an individual is, the closer the two are. Children are pure but completely immature, which is why their parents need to guide them to find lasting happiness. Adults, on the other hand, tend to lose the purity of innocence as years go by, and that makes enjoying the moments harder for them – at least without any mind-altering substances.

These two aspects are the reason I have written also a fairy tale for adults (Apsara's Dance). I want to help people to get in touch with the innocence of childhood that makes every moment a wonder. You can start anew every day, still making use of what you have learnt along the way. Ask yourself how you would live today if you were free from the bondages of your past choices. Then start incorporating that into your life in a virtuous way. Create your own fairy tale and you'll notice that you'll attract people with a desire to experience a similar fairy tale in their lives. When you no longer have contradicting desires, life becomes magically enchanting as it is.

Rule nr 2: Be present and aware!

"The greatest thing you'll ever learn is just to love and be loved in return." – Eden Ahbez

There can be failures in loving but there's never a failure in real love. People come into your life for various reasons and seasons. However, the ultimate meaning of every encounter is the same: to help each other to become more aware of our true selves, our souls or whatever you want to call our essence, which is intimately linked to being present in the state of real love.

We try to fulfill the greatest of our needs in various ways – consciously or unconsciously. The more aware we become, the easier it becomes to find sustainable love. The source of sustainable love is inside us, and other people just reflect that to us – some better than others. However, even if being connected to the real – sustainable – love within is the most important thing, romantic and friendship love shared with other love-filled people are gifts to us as human beings. The romantic or friendship love can also become sustainable if we learn to love, first and foremost, our real selves and the real selves of our objects of love. We can then learn to love others without any other needs than just sharing the air we breathe. Sure we can also enjoy our bodies and minds with each other but we don't need them to fulfill anything in us.

Exceptional loving becomes possible through awareness and presence, which are skills that can be trained. Meditation helps in learning to become present and mindful, which is why in the next section of the book, CONTEMPLATION AND MEDITATION, I have described you many different ways to meditate so that you can find at least one that resonates with you.

I believe it will take me this lifetime to excel in loving and that is why the meaning of my life is to aim for awareness through and for love. What is a perfect lover to you? Why don't you try becoming that for yourself?

Rule nr 3: Challenge yourself gently!

"What's money? A man is a success if he gets up in the morning and goes to bed at night and in between does what he wants to do."
– Bob Dylan

By now you have probably realized that earthly pleasures alone will not make you feel like you live your life to the fullest, so you might be ready to embrace spirituality. Spirituality gives meaning to life but what does it mean? With spirituality life makes more sense – it actually adds the sixth sense to your life. Spirit is the source of inner strength, joy and energy that we need in order to live a thriving life. Therefore, it is important to start your day by connecting to the Source.

It's as if you are a laptop that can be charged during the night. In the morning you decide whether you want to stay connected to the Source via the cable or whether you will use up the stored energy. If you keep connected to the Source, you don't lose your charge during the day. You just need to keep checking that the cable stays attached while you are out and about. There are also differences in batteries in regards to how long they last without the connection to the Source.

I have been talking about different ways of finding the joy and keeping the joy in mind in everyday life, and I have urged you to write down what works for you. Now I go one step further by asking you to describe your Source. What is your God or Soul like? What is the basis of all your beliefs? I ask this because I believe that the more real it becomes to you, the stronger its positive impact on your practical living will be.

In addition to visualizing your Spirit, I encourage you to start writing a spiritual diary because the key to genuine change is awareness. There isn't just one way of doing it, experiment with what works for you. Through jotting down how much attention you give to the spiritual aspect of your life, how much sleep you get, what kind of food you eat, how much you exercise and what virtues you are developing, you will naturally start to increase the balance in your life. Don't forget to add how much fun you have and what is fun for you!

Don't blame yourself if you are not happy with the chart you get when you start. Just be proud of yourself, because you are doing something in order to take better care of yourself by honestly examining yourself and being willing to change. Challenge yourself gently, otherwise you'll get overwhelmed, and feeling discouraged you'll stop before any permanent change has occurred.

Rule nr 4: Find your soul!

"We have different gifts, according to the grace given to each of us. If your gift is prophesying, then prophesy in accordance with your faith; if it is serving, then serve; if it is teaching, then teach; if it is to encourage, then give encouragement; if it is giving, then give generously; if it is to lead, do it diligently; if it is to show mercy, do it cheerfully."
– Romans 12:6-8

So often in the spiritual circles you hear two swearwords: ego and money. Sure, they can restrict one's ability to enjoy life to the fullest, yet on the other hand they are essential as long as we are a part of any society and we have not yet reached the full independence of the soul. Having enough money and strong enough ego aim at independence, which is vital for a balanced life. However, once you have become independent, you should strive towards interdependence. We all have an equally important task to perform in this society; we are to glorify God with our lives. In addition to our unique talents, God has given us the capacity to love, and it is our common duty to develop the skill of loving.

Real independence doesn't mean that we have to live alone and that we shouldn't need other people for anything, even if we should strive to minimize our needs (Buddhism) or fulfill them ourselves (NVC). We certainly shouldn't *expect* others to fulfill our needs. However, outwardly we can never be fully independent, or maybe it is possible for a very handy and balanced person in a paradise island rich in fruit, vegetables and fresh water. Therefore, instead of outer independence, the focus should be in reaching the independence of soul and creating positive connections to other people in this world – and why not other worlds too!

How to reach the independence of soul then? There are many different ways to get there but they all aim at getting to know one's soul, which, in turn, means time spent in some kind of meditation and introspection. Then after one has grasped the nature of one's soul, one should aim at bridging the gap between ego and soul by transforming ego to support the flourishing of one's soul.

Yoga gives great tools for this. As one learns proper breathing, exercises and rests enough, eats healthy and energizing food and can control one's mind, one has reached the real independence that brings freedom and joy into one's life. Then it is time for this independent soul to help the other souls to reach their full bloom and make this world the blossoming reciprocal paradise it could be.

Rule nr 5: Discover the timeless you!

"Who you are transcends space, time, and cause-and-effect."
– Deepak Chopra

I have realized if one is able to connect with the soul of another person, one doesn't need years in order to get to know that person, it is instant. Of course one needs time in order to know the mundane things about the person and his/her likes, as well as how his/her painful memories are stored in the body and mind of that particular person and what triggers it, but the most beautiful and important things one can find out instantly. You either get each other or you don't, and that's apparent right away. You can also find out immediately whether your souls feel at home with each other or not. You also find out instantly whether there is a biological connection between you two – do his/her pheromones entice you? And do you click on a mental level?

Where things go wrong is that our needs can fog our perception on some or all levels. Let's say for example that you just hunger for human touch. Then you meet someone who is interested in you but without your lack of the company of another human being you wouldn't be interested in that person – your biological compatibility is not ideal.

Personally the need to believe good about other people has many times fogged my perception. That is why even if one believes in having connected with the other person's soul, people have to spend time together doing mundane things. It is also important to observe how the person you are interested in interacts with different kinds of people, children, animals and the nature. Actions, not words, reveal the real character.

Before finding that someone to do mundane things with, think what kind of person you would like to be in practice. Then work on becoming that and you'll attract similar kind of people to you.

We have various roles in this life. We use them like clothes. Today I will wear my writer role. How do writers dress? For me it's something comfortable like woolly socks, cozy pants and a wrap in wintertime. Yesterday I was a dance and yoga teacher; a training outfit. Tomorrow I'll have some important business meetings; a suit. And so on. I believe some people are happier with fewer roles, whereas other people need more variety. It might be harder for a person with fewer roles to accept that the roles are not the whole picture, whereas for someone with many roles it's impossible to believe that a single role would capture the reality as it is. Ultimately, all of us need to learn to love ourselves with and without the roles we play.

How can we love ourselves? By honestly examining ourselves and facing everything we discover without positive or negative judgment. There is always someone who is better or worse than we are on the ego level, but we are all equal on the soul level. There is a place for all of us here with the skills, talents and attributes we have at the moment. If we want to change from this place to another, we first need to accept where and how we are now, only then a genuine change can happen.

Don't resist - embrace yourself and life! Enjoy the fact that you can play many different roles like you were acting on stage. If you happen to play your role badly, don't worry, it is just one of the roles you play, not the whole truth about you.

Rule nr 6: Embrace the real needs!

"We never understand how little we need in this world until we know the loss of it" – J. M. Barrie

I found myself utterly contented as the month of April turned into May, my beloved birth month. The sun is shining again and flowers and leaves are starting to bloom. I bought some fresh herbs and placed them on the windowsill. Life. The hibernation is over and I feel alive again together with my environment.

All this made me realize how great is my need for the sun and warmth in keeping me contented, and I decided to re-read Maslow's theory on the hierarchy of needs.

Abraham Maslow first introduced the theory in *"A Theory of Human Motivation"* in 1943. Maslow studied what he called exemplary people such as Albert Einstein, Jane Addams, and Eleanor Roosevelt, rather than mentally ill or neurotic people. His theory was fully expressed in his 1954 book *"Motivation and Personality."*

Maslow's hierarchy of needs is portrayed in the shape of a pyramid, with the largest and lowest levels of needs at the bottom, and the need for self-actualization at the top. First come the physiological needs like homeostasis (the balance of a particular system like the Earth and a human being), breathing, food, water, excretion, sleep and sex. Then comes the need for safety: security of body, employment, resources, morality, the family, health and property. This is followed by our need for love and belonging, which are fulfilled through friends, family and sexual intimacy. Next ladder portrays the needs for esteem; self-esteem, confidence, achievement, respect of and by others. On top of the hierarchy is the need for self-actualization; morality, creativity, spontaneity, problem solving, lack of prejudice and acceptance of facts.

I wouldn't necessarily see our needs in a hierarchy; I see them as a sum that varies in shape. Sometimes we are desperate to fulfill some of the "higher" needs even if all of the "lower" needs are not met first, and sometimes we don't feel needy at all. Some wisdom traditions teach that we actually have everything we need inside ourselves.

25

There are even examples of people who can go on without food and water for long periods of time, which indicates that there exists a possibility for conquering even the basic human needs.

As I wrote this, I had found a letter to my unborn child, which I had written almost five years prior to that day, and I asked myself why was I still so far away from giving birth to a baby. Then it came to me: my intuition wanted me to develop the motherly aspect of my immortal soul at that particular time in my ego's life. What are the aspects of motherhood that are eternal? Patience for sure, not forgetting unconditional love and wisdom.

The need for offspring could be a call to develop one's maternal or paternal qualities. The need for sexual gratification could be a call to merge completely with the beloved or the Universe. The need for financial support is often a need to experience more safety and security, and so forth. What matters, is that we find all the aspects of our souls and perfect them to the best of our abilities.

I encourage you to allow your intuition to answer you what your real needs are. When you feel a desire arising, ask how you could answer to it on the level of your soul first. Once you have given an answer to that question, your intuition will lead you easily to its manifestation on the ego level as it sees fit.

As you know already, I have now also manifested the most adorable little girl in addition to the qualities I developed while still waiting for her arrival. The qualities have most certainly made the experience of motherhood more peaceful and joyful for me!

Rule nr 7: Experiment on yourself!

"It is only by making physical experiments that we can discover the intimate nature of matter and its potentialities. And it is only making psychological and moral experiments that we can discover the intimate nature of mind and its potentialities. In the ordinary circumstances of average sensual life these potentialities of the mind remain latent and unmanifested. If we would realize them, we must fulfil certain conditions and obey certain rules, which experience has shown empirically to be valid." – Aldous Huxley, The Perennial Philosophy

I forced myself to a human test: I wanted to know how celibacy would influence me. Would it help me to gather more spiritual and emotional clarity?

The results were not as important as the mere observation of what was going on in me. However, I had a strong experience of kundalini rising and found compassion, which to me brings the ultimate clarity in life.

We will never be truly joyful as long as we live from our egos. Egos have been given us in order to work on our karma, to develop our character, to further the evolution of our awareness, in short, to experience this life here on Earth. However, this life is "just" a game, a dream that we are all dreaming. The reality lies beyond this life and that is why we desire to make our lives count for something more than any of our Earthly achievements, experiences or pleasures.

What kind of experiment could be beneficial for you and your surroundings?

Rule nr 8: Be authentic!

"Truth alone is sexy." - Pocholo Martínez Bordiú

It is hard when you sense that someone you love sees something ugly in you. You already know that this imperfection exists in you and when someone you love confirms it, it is amplified ten-folds. The only cure for this is to console yourself with the fact that your loved one is still imprisoned by his/her ego too much to experience the beautiful unconditional love that doesn't care about "imperfections" or that his/her taste is simply different.

Imperfections make us human. They give us character and bring color to our lives. Sharing imperfections builds intimacy. They help us to develop ourselves and our surroundings. Embrace them, don't try to push them away. At the same time cultivate humble wisdom, since arrogance is not sexy either.

I used to be terribly shy and lacking in self-confidence. The best thing that has ever happened to me was when I learnt to love myself unconditionally. So, do as I did: fake it until you make it. Trust that the absolute awareness is guiding you every step of the way and you will never need to lack self-confidence anymore.

Things that I find sexy are things that I also appreciate greatly like authenticity and empathy. Another important factor for sex appeal is self-confidence. Only a person who appreciates him/herself seems genuinely desirable to others. That way you don't have to fulfill any other purpose with lovemaking than just connecting with love and enjoying the process along the way. How can you then make yourself more self-confident?

Here are some tips I have collected over the years to my personal self- confidence bank:

1. Find a hobby that keeps you physically fit → It will help you to function better. You are more able to enjoy lovemaking when you actually have energy for it – and flexibility isn't such a bad thing either. It will also help you to like your own body because you have become team instead of being enemies.

2. Lovemaking builds up self-confidence. → To be loved and to be loving in a physical way has proven out to be healthy in many ways.
3. Increase positive thinking by re-reading the good days in your diary. → We create our lives in our minds.

4. Share your joy with others. → We are social beings and it brings tremendous pleasure to see how we can contribute to the happiness of other people.

5. Challenging yourself is good. → It is very good for self-confidence to step sometimes out of your comfort zone and put your effort into something new without judging how it will go.

6. Dare to be different. → When you embrace yourself as you are, and let go off the "you" you think you should be, you have taken a big step towards building a healthy and sustainable self-confidence.

Rule nr 9: Ask questions!

"The individual, through prolonged psychological disciplines, gives up completely all attachment to his personal limitations, idiosyncrasies, hopes and fears, no longer resists the self-annihilation that is prerequisite to rebirth in the realization of truth, and so becomes ripe, at last, for the great at-one-ment. His personal ambitions being totally dissolved, he no longer tries to live but willingly relaxes to whatever may come to pass in him." – Joseph Campbell, The Hero with a Thousand Faces (p. 204-205)

I ask questions all the time – either from myself or from others because increasing the awareness is my greatest passion – increasing it through and for love specifically. That is why I have asked myself countless times: "How do you know who is The One?"

I have come to the conclusion that, first, you have to know yourself – and that takes a lot of soul searching if you wish to have the correct interpretation. You have to be as honest as possible about who you are and who you want to become. Then, follow your heart. I believe that there are many compatible partners but only one who is the correct one right now.

As the hopeless romantic I am, I make the map of my own life even more challenging by insisting that there exists The One for me. There are many people who have crossed my path before and that is why I feel a greater affinity with some people than others. However, it is only with The One that I have been connected from the beginning of time and will spend the Eternity together. But love life is never simple and straightforward. We keep changing forms but the connection is never lost and every time we learn to read our maps correctly, we find each other again. Every time the encounter is as surprising, magical and beautiful like it would be happening for the first time. Only the feeling of home reveals that we have met countless times before or, rather, we have always been connected but the veil of separation has been lifted – like in the enlightenment.

What are you pondering as we speak? What is the most important question to you right now? What kind of questions are your emotions directing you towards?

Rule nr 10: Know what works for you!

"Because just as winter is followed by spring, nothing comes to an end: after reaching your objective, you have to start again, always using all that you have learnt on the way." – Paulo Coelho

I have realized that in order to live an enjoyable life, what matters the most, is the decision to enjoy the joy. It all starts with a mindset that believes joy is possible everyday. Then in order to feel joyful, what matters are the practical details of how to enjoy one's life.

The transition periods are often in some ways hard to cope with, no matter if we are talking about weather or personal growth. However, right away when we let go of the need to achieve something and concentrate on enjoying the little things in life and seizing the moment, we suddenly realize that we, or our surroundings, have changed into something new, which feels exhilarating. This is *a* time to rejoice and be grateful.

New challenges will occur because they keep us going and experiencing life in different ways. When we are faced with those challenges, we should not moan or complain.

Instead, we should look at them as a puzzle we need to solve. Don't we all love to solve the mysteries with Poirot? Why does it then feel so repulsive to solve our own problems? Because it is "real" and we are afraid that we won't be able to solve the problem, and that we'll make grave mistakes. However, how else do we learn? If we would never encounter our limits, how would we know whether we are on the right track or not?

Yes, negative feelings seem to be a part of life. How could we experience the positive emotions if we wouldn't feel the flip side of the coin? I don't think we could feel all the exhilarating positive emotions without the other end of the continuum, which are the negative emotions. I believe, however, that we could experience a constant serene joy if we would be willing to let go of the hype of the positive feelings that follow, for example, from falling in love.

That serene joy is often called peace of God. It is a place where one can breathe easily. It is easy to feel when one is sitting on a warm Caribbean beach, or standing on a mountain in the Alps. Nature is a source of that serenity. Another place to find that joy is in the arms of someone who loves you and who you love back unconditionally. Or one can feel it after some solitary meditation or prayer time. The ways of finding that joy are endless and depend on who you really are. What makes you tick? What I want to emphasize is that no matter what situation we are faced with, we'd be better off finding the joy in it – that simply makes life more enjoyable.

As strange as it sounds, most of us don't know ourselves. We have all kinds of labels that describe us, but who are we deep down? Truly knowing oneself and learning to love oneself as one is – with warts and all – makes it eventually possible for oneself to enjoy the joy of living. Without knowing oneself, one can have only random moments of joy. However, as one gets to know one's real self, one is able to tap the pool of serene joy whenever needed.

Where does the dissatisfaction in life come from? I believe it comes from not really knowing oneself. If we would know ourselves, we would be able to accept life as it comes and change it gradually to increase the joy. Or we could accept the full responsibility of engaging in ephemeral positive feelings. Taking time to get to know ourselves can feel like a waste but it is not. Many people put so much time into getting to know famous people by gossiping, watching TV programs, reading magazines or using social media. Why wouldn't you put that time into getting to know someone with whom you'll spend the rest of your life?

Rule nr 11: Remember the gratitude attitude!

"The greatest gift you can give another is the purity of your attention." – Richard Moss

I got into the habit of making vision boards after reading Julia Cameron's *The Artist's Way* a few years back. They are not only a great tool for visualizing one's dreams but also for following the fulfillment of them. So easily we forget that the things we take for granted today, first existed only in our dreams. Take extra time this week to appreciate all the existing treasures in your life. What are they?

Are they your home, family, friends, or perhaps a new job, shoes or a book? Maybe you consider as a treasure some words you finally heard after a long waiting period? Or do you treasure your health? Have you reached an objective that has yielded positive influence on a wider scale?

Did you manage to stop a bad habit? Did a stranger smile at you when you needed it most? Our world is filled with treasures, we are all rich with them, we just need to see them and appreciate them as such, and not only run after new treasures all the time.

Remember that the attitude you have when you give presents is at least as important as what you give. Give things out of love, not out of obligation. Don't stress that you will give a wrong gift, you won't if your intention is a positive and unselfish one. Being loving is better present than any gift given with a lot of negative turmoil. If you don't have time to find or the means to give the kind of gifts you'd like to, let the people know your intention creatively – make a poem, sing a song or why not blog about it.

Rule nr 12: See old things with new eyes!

"Countless thousands of couples have discovered that the best sex is experienced within a loving marriage. Such sex goes way beyond physical gratification. It creates a deep emotional, psychological and even spiritual bond which has the power to communicate love in a way that transcends words. Our sexual relationship can express our love for each other tenderly, regularly and passionately over years of married life." – Nicky & Sila Lee (The Marriage Book, p. 275)

Who wouldn't want to be the lover of a lifetime? Yet, most people think that people should know how to make love just by following their instincts. Maybe it could work in the Garden of Eden but it doesn't quite work in our flawed world in which people's instincts get influenced by all kinds of cultural stuff. Therefore, one should study the matter from reliable sources. In their Marriage Book Nicky

& Sila Lee jot down these six factors as the qualities of a great lover: communication, tenderness, responsiveness, romance, anticipation and variety. It's not the size of the penis or the duration of the intercourse that matter so much, or even how often you have sex. Even if Kama sutra does suggest that it makes life easier if the size and the libido of the man and woman match.

Sex as a need has probably always been controversial. Yes, our body is coded to look for an intimate partner in order to reproduce and enjoy along the way. Yet, following blindly the calls of pheromones does not make a person happy - at least not the majority of people. It makes the mind and soul captive to one's body, whereas, what we really want is freedom from all kinds of bondages. This doesn't mean you should repress your sexual urges, quite the contrary. If you try to repress them, they'll only come back stronger and harder to cope with. Again you should embrace yourself as you are.

According to tantric tradition, reaching an orgasm too often is not good. However, tantric tradition doesn't try to fight the sexuality but to channel it differently through increasing awareness and with the practical help of different kinds of yoga and meditation techniques. The sexual energy is a great power that can be channeled into the benefit of the mankind, and it starts with an individual. Learn to control your sexual energy little by little and you'll become free to enjoy love making at its best – fulfilling your needs holistically, and maybe even transforming you and your partner deeply.

Rule nr 13: Clarify your values!

"Happiness is the consequence of personal effort. You fight for it, strive for it, insist upon it, and sometimes even travel around the world looking for it. You have to participate relentlessly in the manifestations of your own blessings. And once you have achieved a state of happiness, you must never become lax about maintaining it..." — *Elizabeth Gilbert, "Eat, Pray, Love"*

Virtuous Arts was established to help people to create and enjoy arts, and that way help joy to spread. It is truly an honor to assist people in dreaming and manifesting their dream lives. Manifesting dreams is not always easy, and I can't give you easy answers and formulas to fulfill your dreams instantly. Patience and individual effort are almost always required. However, the effort can be fun like it is for children to learn to walk, and patience is required less and less if you enjoy the steps along the way to your goal.

It is sometimes hard to balance between developing the egos and not upsetting them too much. I do my best to show that I love and respect the people I teach or consult even if I'm constructively criticizing their actions. People come to me usually to learn or develop a skill or change a life circumstance, which means they want to change, but often times the inner resistance to change still exists strong – at least in the realm of the subconscious.

We are all in the life long school of joy, and developing our egos should always be in the service of increasing virtuous fun in the world. If you have lost sight of the joy, you need to loosen up a bit, or if instead you find yourself getting bored, you'll need to demand more of yourself. You only need to stay aware and present, and you'll be able to maintain the right balance. Knowing your values helps you to know which virtues to concentrate on and what brings you joy.

Here are the ABC of values of Virtuous Arts to help you to clarify yours: Abundance, Beauty, Creativity, Dance, Empowerment, Fitness, Giving, Honesty, Integrity, Joy, Kindness, Love, Motivation, Nobility, Observation, Play, Questioning, Reliability, Spirituality, Thanksgiving, Union, Variety, X factor, Yoga, Zeal.

Rule nr 14: Continue on your chosen path!

Once upon a time there was a boy who met a girl he believed could be The One. Never before had he instantly felt so right about being with someone. He felt that with her his soul was at home at the same time it was traveling to new interesting horizons. This made him peacefully excited. He did not want to mess it all up like all the other relationships before her. Determined to do everything right this time, he went to consult the Wise.

They told him to stay aware and focused on the purity of the feeling he had for her and their possible lifetime – and perhaps even all eternity – together. "Do not get distracted by all the other beautiful souls and bodies you will meet - they have just come into your life to help you stay focused on your Soulmate. When you will catch yourself thinking impure thoughts, let them go and empty your mind. If emptying your mind feels too hard, look at a picture of your loved one and hold the ideal of your soul companionship in your heart. Be merciful to yourself and keep getting up every time you fall short of your ideal. If you do not give up, one day you will wake up your mind and heart fully cleansed from all impurity and then you can enjoy a blissful existence with your Soulmate – provided that she has felt the same about you and put the same effort into developing her virtues."

The boy felt excited about the greatest challenge he had ever been confronted with. Finally he was ready to battle for the Good against the Evil of mediocrity, virtues as his weapon.

The boy who had felt excited about the greatest challenge he had ever been confronted with was beginning to feel weary. His battle for the Good against the Evil of mediocrity, virtues as his weapon, wasn't looking too good. He hardly remembered the time he had been able to share with his princess before going off to the battle.

He had followed the advice from The Wise as best as he had been able to, but staying aware and focused on the purity of the feeling he had for his princess and their possible lifetime - and perhaps even all eternity - together had turned out to be more difficult than he had expected. He had gotten distracted by some other beautiful people he had met in the battlefield and now he felt like he had failed.

But then he looked again a photo of his heart's chosen one and remembered The Wise saying that if he would not give up, one day he would wake up his mind and heart fully cleansed from all impurity and then the blissful existence with his Soulmate would become a possibility. Feeling of home pervaded his whole being as he dreamt about holding her in his arms. Suddenly it became clear to him that the war here was over for him and, with the courage he had gathered during the battles, he would now enable him to fight for the heart of his princess in her presence. It was time for him to return and declare his love for her.

How she would respond to his declaration, and what would happen afterwards, was impossible to know but he knew that this leap of faith would help him in developing his virtues no matter what the result would be.

Rule nr 15: Picture your life!

"Will you do something for me, please? Just picture your life for me? 30 years from now, 40 years from now? What's it look like?" - The Notebook by Nicholas Sparks

One of the most exciting times in my life is when I start a new notebook. I just got a beautiful notebook as a Christmas gift, and I've been sniffing it and holding it in my hands like it was a long lost lover. To start a new notebook is a kind of a holy moment for me. I feel awe in the presence of the blank papers. I believe that it is always a start of a new path and how I begin, is highly significant. This belief makes me humble and excited about the mystery that will gradually unfold on the pages.

I want to find the right kind of meditative quotation that will pave the way for a richer future. Maybe I will write my motto in life – lighten up to be enlightened – on the first page so that the notebook will be true to my real self and will support my mission – increasing the awareness through and for love. I could also add the title of my blog – enjoying the joy – and the name of my company – virtuous arts – to the first page because I still wish to continue to create and enjoy the joy through virtuous arts.

Picture now your life in your new notebook or in My Notes section at the end of this book.

II CONTEMPLATION AND MEDITATION (Certainty)

Four monks decided to meditate silently without speaking for two weeks. By nightfall on the first day, the candle began to flicker and then went out. The first monk said, "Oh, no! The candle is out." The second monk said, "Aren't we not supposed to talk?" The third monk said, "Why must you two break the silence?" The fourth monk laughed and said, "Ha! I'm the only one who didn't speak."
– Gene Torisky

Now that you know yourself and the world a bit better, it is time to ask for what you like and then rest – both physically and mentally.

Rule nr 16: Seek Divine Wisdom!

"What lies behind us and what lies before us are tiny matters compared to what lies within us." – Ralph Waldo Emerson

What kind of life would you like to lead? Can you imagine it in positive terms? If you can, it is only a matter of time that the steps to your goal will reveal themselves if you are able to free yourself from your blocks and be fully present in every moment of your life.
We will come back to dealing with blocks later on but now I'd like to concentrate on the positive aspect of putting imagination into practice.

I believe that psychic abilities – that could help you achieve the dreams your imagination has come up with – may be achieved by anyone who learns the proper mental and physical discipline. What is needed, is the pure desire – *kundalini.*

Kundalini resides in the sacrum bone in three and a half coils. Yoga proposes that this energy can be "awakened" by a guru (spiritual teacher), but body and spirit must be prepared by yogic austerities such as pranayama (or breath control), physical exercises (like the asanas of hatha yoga), visualization, meditation and chanting. Kundalini can also awaken spontaneously, for example through love, serving people and through some intense experiences, such as childbirth.

Kundalini is considered an interaction of the subtle body along with chakra energy centers and nadis channels. Each chakra is said to contain special characteristics and with proper training, moving kundalini energy through these chakras can help express or open these characteristics. When kundalini awakes, it forces a passage through a hollow canal, and as it rises step by step, layer after layer of the mind becomes open and all the different visions and wonderful powers come to the Yogi. When it reaches the brain, the Yogi is perfectly detached from the body and mind and the soul finds itself free.

The arousing of kundalini is said by some to be the one and only way of attaining Self-Realization or Self-Knowledge, which is considered equivalent to Divine Wisdom. Divine Wisdom brings the aspirant pure joy, pure knowledge and pure love, which ultimately lies at the core of every dream. Or am I wrong?

Rule nr 17: Concentrate on something noble!

*"Thoughts of love, peace, contentment, purity, perfection, Divinity, will make you, and also others around you, perfect and Divine." –
Swami Sivananda*

The theoretical framework for happiness is easy, it is the practice where many stumble. Therefore, we will concentrate now on the practical side of joy. Knowledge, awareness about yourself and your surroundings, is crucial in order to act in a constructive way.

How then do we increase our wisdom? Through meditation. There is a law of mind that says that if a thought or an idea prevails in mind, all the other thoughts and ideas gradually have the tendency to submit to the prevailing thought/idea. This is the basic principle of meditation. I think it is because of this that many religions urge one to believe only in one good God and think of Him at all times.

The prevailing thought is created by concentration, and the movement of the mind around that particular thought is meditation. Therefore, concentrate on something noble, and when your mind wanders away, bring it back gently. Our mind is unruly by nature but when we manage to tame our own mind, its power becomes enormous. Healthy life style, virtuous inputs, proper food and exercise are some things that can help us to concentrate on "our God".

Meditation does not need to happen sitting quietly, eyes closed and repeating OM in one's mind. That works for some people, for others meditation may come easier while listening to a beautiful piece of music or watching one's beloved at sleep. Your actual thought is not important. The main thing is the purity - or absence – of thought.

1st Meditation Practice:

Tonight when you go to sleep go through the day with the lenses of love, peace, contentment, purity, perfection and Divinity. If you find it hard, then just thank for the day and trust that it was perfect even if you can't see it that way right now. Then release it by saying something like: "May everything work for the highest good of everyone concerned!"

After that you can start visualizing the next day with the lenses of love, peace, contentment, purity, perfection and Divinity. Think of all the things that you know will happen and see yourself being fully present in them.

When you reach a positive state, you can let go of all thoughts and just enjoy the lightness of being.

Rule nr 18: Clear your mind!

"Every saint has a past and every sinner has a future." – Oscar Wilde

When one is striving to become more virtuous, one might not always *feel* joyful. The individual effort is an effort but the joy after the effort is worth it. Especially because when a person is fully virtuous – a saint – the joy is constant.
I truly believe that it is our vices that make us miserable. Or rather the dissonance between the knowledge about virtues and putting them in practice. When one has enough wisdom to see the right conduct but not the temperance to yield to it, one experiences discomfort. Then again, if someone hasn't received any virtuous education, that person might be happy to lead an immoral life. Yet, it is not true joy and it can be taken away any moment the objects that bring happiness are taken away. Think of bullies for example, they can seem happy with their power but they are in a constant state of fear of losing it.

According to some studies, it seems that temperance is the hardest virtue to develop for human beings. Why do you think this is so? I believe the answer lies in the fact that in Heaven we don't need to practice temperance because we would automatically know the right amount of food, exercise, rest and play we need – like animals do.

I actually feel like it comes down to the individual effort of clearing and controlling the mind through concentration and meditation. The mind can help us to develop our virtues by helping us to see whether our thoughts and actions are helping or hindering us in our virtuous pursuits, and the more virtuous we are, the easier it is for us to truly stay in the present moment of beauty, love, creativity, joy and inner peace. Just don't trust the mind blindly before it is completely and constantly pure.

2nd Meditation Practice:

Pay attention to your feelings. Are you feeling angry, sad, happy, excited or ashamed for example? Now can you just accept your feelings as they are without trying to find a reason for them? Can you be with them without trying to interpret them? Can you spot where in your body you feel sensations and what kind of sensations do you feel? Now breathe in deeply in through your nose allowing your abdomen to come out, breathe out slowly mouth open and the belly goes in. Repeat this at least three more times. You can also add the sound "Aah!" when breathing out, if you wish to feel more relaxed. How do you feel now? Do you feel any different?

"Memory is always faulty. Emotions are always true."

Rule nr 19: Understand your true nature!

"It's not who you are that holds you back, it's who you think you're not." - Anonymous

I used to lack self-confidence, which is a positively realistic attitude. When I formulated a dream and focused on it, I started to feel like I wasn't good enough or really worthy of reaching the goal. Why was that? There were many possible reasons for it, ranging from my past experiences, my personality, an in-built trait of all people to the possibility of our society wanting women to feel inferior to men or young people to old people etc. The right question wasn't really why I lacked self-confidence, but what the lack of self-confidence was telling me and how I was I able to change it.

As I see it, self-confidence comes down to feeling worthy of love. How can we be worthy of love? We are simply born into this world. We can't buy or manipulate self-confidence. Self-confidence is your birthright sprouting from the love that created you. You are loved, therefore you are.

By making ourselves more lovable to ourselves, we make it easier for us to feel worthy and accept love. However, the real self-confidence comes when we understand our true nature through meditation. Meditation brings you into connection with your soul. It helps you to remember that you are not your thoughts or your body. You experience life through them but you are infinitely something more - your unique soul.

3rd Meditation Practice:

Do this meditation in the morning as you are making yourself to look your best to the world. As you are washing your face and putting on make-up/shaving your face, think beautiful thoughts.

What nice do you have to say about yourself? Don't pay attention to your tiredness and so-called flaws. Instead, compliment yourself for getting up from bed and taking care of your hygiene for the wellbeing of everyone around you. Think positively about the people you are going to meet and the tasks that you are about to perform. Think how smoothly your transportation to your work place will go. Come up with something good about the current weather (This is a tough one in Finland in November!).

Thank for the chance to make a positive difference in the world around you. Lastly, look yourself in the mirror and tell your soul that you love it and you will do your best to enrich it.

Rule nr 20: Find sustainable energy!

"We believe we must get attention, love, recognition, support, approval – all forms of energy – from others. We adopt a way to pull the energy in our direction by the kind of interactions we had as children with our parents." – James Redfield

Control drama is a concept I first encountered years back in the novel "The Celestine Prophecy" by James Redfield. Control dramas are examples of negative patterns that tend to occur when people are not aware. People very often feel lack of energy and due to that they try to compete for it with others. We learn our control dramas as children in interactions with out family members who are trying to pull energy out of us. In the novel Redfield categorizes the control dramas into four groups: Intimidator, Interrogator, Aloof and Poor Me. Most of us have one dominant way of manipulating energies even if some people use different combinations of all of these in different circumstances.

*"**Intimidators** get everyone to pay attention to them by force of loudness, physical strength, threats, unexpected outbursts. ... They make you feel afraid or anxious. ... They initially engage others by creating an aura of power. ... As you strive to prove yourself or answer to [**Interrogators**], the more energy you send their way. ...*

Hypervigilant, their behavior may range from being cynical, skeptical, sarcastic, needling, perfectionistic, self-righteous, to viciously manipulative. They initially engage others with their wit, infallible logic, facts, and intellect. ... Aloof people are caught up in their own internal world of unresolved struggles, fears, and self-doubt. ...

Their behavior ranges from disinterested, unavailable, uncooperative, to condescending, rejecting, contrary, and sneaky. ... They initially engage through their mysterious, hard-to-get persona. ... Always pessimistic, Poor Me's pull attention to themselves by worried facial expressions, sighing, trembling, crying, staring into the distance, answering questions slowly, and retelling poignant dramas and crises. ... Poor Me's initially seduce by their vulnerability and need for help."

The starting point for overcoming the control dramas is, of course, becoming aware of them, accepting them, and then finding more sustainable ways to gain energy. A great way to gain inner energy without taking away from others, is through meditation. Just paying attention to your breathing like I instructed in the 2nd meditation practice, and how it affects your body, is a good starting point for becoming centered internally and having sustainable energy at your disposal.

Then from this place of stillness the negative control dramas can be changed into positive personal traits: the intimidators can become a source of power not only for themselves but also for others; the interrogators can use their intellect and wit to benefit themselves and others; the aloof can bring depth and meaning to our lives; and poor me's can increase intimacy by being vulnerable.

I have talked here how energy can be found inside oneself and sustained through awareness. It is important to make ourselves aware also physically. Changing the negative control dramas into positive personal traits starts with taking the responsibility for our own feelings and actions.

Hence, our minds can help our energy levels to stay up. We can also forget the mind and work straight with our bodies. Many people have experienced how physical exercises actually give energy rather than take. Yoga is definitely a form of exercise that increases the positive energy for one to function as a balanced person in changing circumstances.

Yoga postures focus first on the health of the spine, its strength and flexibility, because the spinal column houses the all-important nervous system. By maintaining the spine's flexibility and strength through exercise, circulation is increased and the nerves are ensured their supply of nutrients and oxygen. When the nervous system is working well, the body stays better under mind's control and helps the practitioner to stay healthy.

When your body is healthy, it is easier for you to stay centered and give good energy to everyone you meet. Life is about experiencing the love that unites us all. Learn to tap into the pulse of life by keeping your life simple.

Rule nr 21: Be silent and breathe!

"The dramatic psychological shift that occurs whenever we fall in love is actually a temporary state of spiritual liberation, a glimpse of who you really are." – Deepak Chopra

You don't need an outer other half in order to fall in love, you can fall in love alone. When you honestly think about it, whenever you have fallen in love with someone, have you really fallen in love with the person as he or she is, or have you fallen for some missing piece in your life and built a story around it? Therefore, it is important to find

48

the Love within before you can truly fall in love with someone else. I know, it doesn't always feel so easy!

How can one love oneself in a society where nothing is good enough? Just pause for a second now. What would be good enough for you today and in thirty years' time? Most likely the honest answer is that you don't know. How could we know when most of us have only vague ideas about what we like now let alone tomorrow or in ten years' time?

Behind all the moving attributes, however, lies an unchangeable core and that is unconditional love or soul as some people call it. Therefore, you will have to connect with your soul in order to find love, truth and meaning in this life. How to do that? Be silent, meditate, breath in, breath out and smile. Then act.
If you don't know how to act from the place of serene joy, ask advice from wiser people. Read books, listen to talks, and converse with people you think have got it right.

You can be in love at all times, the joy of love is always in your reach. Like any other skill, it only takes practice to tap into that blissful state we call love.

4th Meditation Practice:

Think of someone you love. Think what makes him or her feel loved. Can you do that to him/her today? If not, is there someone else who could do that or something similar you could do? What sacrifices you need to make in order to do that? Can you do them with a light heart? If so go ahead, if not, think why the sacrifice is so huge for you. Maybe you need to love yourself first? Think what makes you feel loved? Can you do that for yourself now?

Rule nr 22: Balance your life for health!

"Health is a state wherein all organs function perfectly under the intelligent control of the mind." – International Sivananda Yoga Vedanta Centers

Health is something one starts to think about in the absence of it, and this is not so common when we are young. However, I have always been intrigued by health. One of my favourite reading as a child was four heavy volumes of a series of books on alternative healing called *"Terveen elämän salaisuudet"* meaning The Secrets of Healthy Life. The mystery involved in being healthy fascinated me. There were so many ways to take care or heal oneself.

For a little girl the perfect health seemed to come down to healthy mind and that is why I thought I wanted to become a psychiatrist for a long time. However, at some point I experienced a political awakening and I felt that actually our surroundings influence greatly how healthy our minds can be and, very modestly, I decided to change the structures of the society instead so that nobody would have to visit a psychiatrist in the utopia we would create!

How to get to that healthy utopia then? Philosophy, arts and religion clarify to us in what kind of utopia we would be like to live in, then it is up to politicians, engineers, doctors and others to make it into a practical reality, and again for teachers to pass the information on to the next generation.

Yoga philosophy is the most holistic and practical one I have encountered so far. Swami Vishnu-Devananda, one of my gurus, has said that *"Health is wealth. Peace of mind is happiness. Yoga shows the way."* Yoga teaches that if a person lives against the natural laws, he or she becomes ill.

Similarly, if a person violates the ethical principles, he or she will suffer. With ethical principles I mean one's own principles. I believe that if one's action differs from one's ethical principles, one will eventually feel uncomfortable. Then when that dissonance is prolonged and not solved, one can become sick – either mentally or physically. How one can solve the dissonance can happen either through changing one's actions or ethical principles, or simply through accepting the dissonance. Generally it seems easier to change actions than genuinely change one's principles.

In the need of inspiration, I opened again one of my favorite books *"The Artist's Way"* by Julia Cameron, and one sentence triggered my attention: *"we often resist what we most need."* Past week I felt like so many things were hard work. Not just work but communicating with people and performing the mundane routine things one has to do, like cleaning, grocery shopping, paying bills etc. I felt like I wanted to have a holiday from life, or rather, a part of me wanted to continue the holiday I had had a week earlier.

Why was my vacation so lovely? I didn't have to push myself to do anything, everything just flowed. I woke up when I wanted to, I did things I wanted to, and I went to sleep when I wanted to. So, it was the freedom of choice and the abundance of time that made life beautiful. After my week off I could have still declined to go back to work but it would have had consequences that I would have had to deal with. Responsibility can sometimes feel heavy. But if I hadn't fulfilled my responsibilities well prior to my holiday, I wouldn't have been able to enjoy the holiday so much.

I believe we all need both, responsibility and freedom, but for some people responsibility is more important than freedom and vice versa. I think that my natural inclination is towards freedom, therefore, restrictions that come from responsibility can sometimes feel overwhelming. Especially when I know how to use my freedom in a responsible yet unconventional way. I suppose *"we often resist what we most need"* would in my case mean that, if I would like to develop as a human being, I should increase my responsibilities instead of the freedom I crave. What is the thing that you resist the most right now and can you see that embracing it could improve the balance of your life?

So, we come back to the importance of growing awareness. If we don't know the natural laws, ethical principles and the right balance, we can stay healthy and happy with luck but if we know them, we can slowly learn how to live accordingly without even thinking about them.
I believe that health is the building block of joy, and awareness is the foundation of health.

Rule nr 23: Know your boundaries!

"It is impossible for you to do what is right in your heart and it's wrong for someone else. One right action is right for the whole world. Come to this place of knowing exactly what you are not and rest in completely in what you are. That's the innocence in you. When you come to this place, everything flows for you." – Mooji

When I wrote this a very dear friend of mine had just had her first baby. Witnessing that beautiful miracle of life had reminded me of my aim to become a writer mom. I had been conscious of that desire for at least ten years by that time. I had had other interests as well, which had probably side-tracked me every now and then, but had still been complementary to these goals.

I had been trying to find the right steps to reach this aim by planning many different scenarios after it didn't happen naturally with my ex-husband. As I was writing this I realized that I wouldn't find the answers by trying to think through all the options. I just had to find myself. I had got lost in my thoughts, thinking what I needed to do, what other people expected of me etc. I realized that those thoughts and expectations were not me. In order to find the real me, I just needed to relax and breathe. By concentrating on my breathing and getting aware of my body, I would get in touch with the real me again.

Then, from this genuine place of being, I asked what is my real goal in life? To increase my awareness through and for love, and lighten up to be enlightened, which I had thought would manifest itself the best as a writer mom. When I concentrated my attention on what should my life look like? Light, full of committed love and creativity. Was it like that then? No. Why? Because I was trying to make decisions that would allow my life to look like that instead of just being light, fully committed to creativity and love.

I believed that my life could be light and full of love right then – even without my own child and an established career as a writer if, instead of trying to convince myself and others, I would have just accepted myself and my situation as it was. Why was I then making it harder for myself? Why was it so hard to accept myself and my situation? Because I wanted proof that I was worthy of reaching my aim. In order to love myself, I thought that I had to make everyone else happy first. I believed other people when they said that only *I* can make them happy, even if deep down I knew it was not true. My insecure ego just wanted to feel loved and listened to those cries like the word of God.

So, in order to get back to the flow, I needed to do right actions or refrain from actions altogether. Not to listen to what other people wanted or what they thought I wanted and needed. I needed to focus on self-love and respect.

When I now concentrate my attention on what should my life look like? Light, full of committed love and creativity. Is it that now? Yes! And I am also a writer-mom!

Rule nr 24: Keep travelling!

"the only thing that is ultimately real about your journey is the step that you are taking at this moment" - Eckhart Tolle

A friend of mine asked me why on the one hand we want to share the rest of our lives with one special person and on the other nothing seems to be good enough for us? I have talked about this before but let's look at it from a new angle today.

Life has many metaphors and a journey is one of them. Do you like traveling alone or with a friend or with a beloved? I guess I belong to the group who would say I like them all, which means that if I would be in a relationship, I would prefer space from my beloved to spend time also alone and with my friends. Yet nothing beats a romantic holiday with your one and true love; time to stare into each others' eyes and merge into one entity, lose boundaries and dive into euphoria.

However, finding that special someone is not that important to me and my friend because we enjoy being alone and with our friends, as well as our childhood family members. It is due to this non-urgency to find a mate that makes us picky – or to lose our interest quickly when we discover something in the potential mate that we think would create unnecessary problems in the long run. I don't see this as a negative thing. I think this is a great opportunity to work on ourselves – finding the wholeness first and foremost as an individual.

Then hopefully one day we'll meet another whole human being who has individually grown into the same direction as we have. However, if we would not ever meet The Travel Partner, that wouldn't matter too much in the end, because we would have enjoyed the journey anyway.

So my friend, instead of concentrating on the fact that you haven't met The Travel Partner yet, enjoy the joy – find the joy in the details of your life right now and keep travelling!

5th Meditation Practice:

Do you like to travel on foot? Let's try today a walking meditation in nature for at least twenty minutes. You can choose a spot that is convenient to you or particularly close to your heart. I could choose to walk by a river, in a forest or in a botanical garden for example.

Then when you walk there, you can first concentrate again on breathing in the fresh air and breathe slowly out all the toxins.

After that you can concentrate on counting your steps. How far did you get before you started thinking about something else? Try again.

Lastly, concentrate on the beauty around you. There is always something beautiful in our surroundings. What is it for you today?

Rule nr 25: Enjoy the joy!

"But let there be spaces in your togetherness and let the winds of the heavens dance between you. Love one another but make not a bond of love: let it rather be a moving sea between the shores of your souls."
– Kahlil Gibran

Following your dreams will bring you to the path of self-discovery and spiritual growth, which will lead to freedom and real love, manifesting itself as creative enjoyment of the joy. Before you can make any major decisions about the course of your life, you'll have to get to know and love your real self. Learn how to increase your wisdom and capacity to love and be loved in return.

What we are looking for is actually inside ourselves but, when we are not mature enough to admit it or not spiritually developed enough to practically manifest it, we use relationships or career or material things to mirror those underdeveloped aspects of our psyches. Loving someone else helps us to love ourselves and brings us closer to the realization that we *are* love and therefore we do not lack anything.

One can manifest one's dreams by changing either one's character or one's circumstances. Complications will occur. Don't give up – continue on your chosen path committed to your goals but flexible in your approach. Develop your self-discipline and mercy. The theoretical framework for finding the love within is easy, it is the rigorous daily practice of virtues that makes it challenging. Just know that the questions are answered when you will find the love within, and the conflicts will be resolved through trusting in life and surrendering to the Divine Love – or whatever you want to call it. Discover your faith and find true love in the process of following your dreams.

True love brings happiness without any reason. True love is pure and perfect without owning anyone or achieving anything. True love brings passion and peace for life at the same time. Life becomes a dance when you connect with your soul and lose yourself in the joy of the moment. Finally there will not be anything in the way of enjoying the joy. Just keep listening to the music!

Rule nr 26: Keep knowing and uncertainty in balance!

"Life is like an ice-cream. Enjoy it before it melts."

I have always thought that the joy one feels when infatuated should be more or less our natural state of being. It makes people naturally optimistic: *"a limerent person tends to emphasize what is admirable in the limerent object."* Balance of hope and uncertainty is what keeps limerence alive and when we think about it, isn't that what life should be all about.

We should never lose hope and, yet, we can never be sure of anything in life, except Love. With Love I mean God or whatever represents the ultimate goodness and bliss. Love is said to give us hope and help to cope with uncertainty. What is it in Love that makes these things happen? I would say it is the soul connection. As one is connected to one's soul, one is connected to Love and then everything makes sense and one feels euphoric.

There are different ways of connecting with one's soul. One of them is love, which goes through different stages; starting from attraction, heightening in infatuation or limerence, continuing to courtship and possibly reaching the life-transforming intimacy. As one has entered the intimacy one should still work to maintain the positive energy of infatuation. In order to evoke the desired energy in the latter, naturally calmer, state of love, one has to learn to play with the feminine and the masculine energies.

Rule nr 27: Meditate with virtuous art!

"Art washes away from the soul the dust of everyday life." – Pablo Picasso

When I was younger I didn't know how to enjoy arts the way I do nowadays. I think it was because I was in such a hurry to live and learn. My French teacher in Paris said to me that you're so young, that's why you are in a hurry.
I didn't understand it then but I do now. *"Hurrying is the flesh trying to do more than the spirit is leading it to do" - Joyce Meyer*

I feel like I have found myself and developed my skills enough to be able to enjoy whatever comes along thoroughly. In short, I believe that I have developed a healthy self-esteem that allows me to enjoy art and not to go to art museums in order to learn something or become more sophisticated. I also acknowledge now that I don't have to see all the paintings in a museum or to spend time with the pieces I don't find interesting. Looking at one painting and achieving a meditative state whilst immersed in it is more than enough. Art does indeed wash away the dust of everyday life from the soul if we let it.

Paulo Coelho quite recently quoted Kandinsky on his blog: *"Art is a power that should be aimed at developing the soul. If art does not do this job, the abyss that separates us from God is left without a bridge. The artist owes his talent to God and has to settle this debt. To do this, he has to work hard, know that he is free in his art but not in his commitment to life. Everything he feels and thinks is part of the raw material with which to improve the spiritual atmosphere around him. Beauty, whether in art or in a woman, cannot be empty; it has to be at the service of humankind and the world."*

This represents my concept of virtuous arts - arts that fill our hearts and minds with good and noble. Art to me is a dynamic concept, which is supposed to live and develop at all times. However, it should not violate the subjective right of a human being or an animal to life. A virtuous artist produces virtuous arts naturally and the virtuous audience is invigorated by it. For me the role of arts can vary; arts can bring aesthetic pleasure to the viewer or listener, they can bring about revelations, they can shake the current concepts of thought and social order, they can bring peace.

Arts are closely linked to our emotions. What emotions did you experience the last time you enjoyed arts?

Rule nr 28: Meditate with quotes!

"Observing that all change is based on nonchange is tremendously important. It points out that your existence, which is enmeshed in change, must be rooted in a deeper state of being that never changes."
— Deepak Chopra

Love makes it possible for us to start anew again and again. It takes time for the body to adapt to changes, so bear with any New (Year's) Resolution at least three months and see how you feel then before quitting frustrated about not seeing any results. It is also worth stopping to reflect back every once in a while. Sometimes even a significant change is difficult to see when you're the work in progress, constantly changing. Give your body, soul and mind plenty of time to adapt to a new lifestyle and enjoy the continuous birth of you.

According to Christianity, you don't need to deserve the redemption in any way, you just need to accept it. Why is it so hard for people to accept the free gift of love? Love can be a terrifying experience because it reveals that ego's certainty is an illusion:

"If you follow love, your life will become uncertain, and the ego craves certainty. You will have to surrender to another person, and the ego prizes its own will above anyone else's. Love will make your feelings ambiguous, and the ego wants to feel the certainty of right and wrong. Many of her experiences that cannot be comprehended by ego apply to love – a lover is confused, spontaneous, vulnerable, exposed, detached, carefree, wondrous, and ever new." – Deepak Chopra

Here are other quotes to contemplate on so that you can allow the magic happen:

"Our disposable culture has taught us to believe that transformative love is the stuff of fairy tales, but nothing could be further from the truth. From the very beginning, we humans were built to love, to be loved, and to be transformed by love." – Gregory K. Popcak in "The Exceptional Seven Percent: The Nine Secrets of the Worlds Happiest Couples."

"Choosing self-love challenges the collective paradigm of guilt and shame that has controlled us for thousands of years. ... If we go the route of the ego, we'll never feel worthy of self-love. If we choose to live our Spirit, we'll be instantly liberated." – Sonia Choquette

"Embracing paradox is a way to move beyond our conditioned controlled worldview. It opens our consciousness into an acceptance of the mystery and uncertainty of life, and that unpredictability is part of what makes life so interesting, fun, and beautiful." – D. Chopra

"You will be bathed in the ocean of bliss when all thoughts are extirpated. This state is indescribable. You will have to feel it yourself."– Sri Swami Sivananda (Thought Power)

"If you could only keep quiet, clear of memories and expectations, you would be able to discern the beautiful pattern of events. It's your restlessness that causes chaos." – Nisargadatta Maharaj

"What really matters is not what function you fulfill in this world, but whether you identify with your function to such an extent that it takes you over and becomes a role that you play. When you play roles you are unconscious. When you catch yourself playing a role, that recognition creates a space between you and the role" – Eckhart Tolle

"Simplicity is the final achievement. After one has played a vast quantity of notes and more notes, it is simplicity that emerges as the crowning reward of art." – Frederic Chopin

Rule nr 29: Meditate your intuition to fruition!

"Really important meetings are planned by the souls long before the bodies see each other." — Paulo Coelho (Eleven Minutes)

Isn't it so that we crave to have beauty and meaning in our lives? Especially on special days like the Valentine's Day we want to experience something magical. Where most people go wrong is that they expect other people or external things to do the trick. The attention is diverted away from oneself, like with the control dramas.

I like that quote from Paulo Coelho because it gives importance to both – the soul and the body – but in the right order. However, most people never let their souls to dream the most beautiful dreams to reality because their minds are in a hurry to fix things to fulfill the needs of the body. They are trying to rationalize instead of following their heart, intuition or whatever you'd like to call the invisible guidance that most of us have sometimes felt.

I remember that when I was younger it was very hard for me to understand the concept of listening to my heart. I felt like my heart was mute and the only irrational guidance I could "hear" came from the pheromones. The talk of the pheromones was the instinctual guidance of being a human, but it had nothing to do with the romantic guidance of the heart that I was encouraged to listen to. It was only through learning to meditate and enjoy staying still that I started to trust the voice of my gentle heart. The voice was very quiet to begin with but nowadays it is very clear, and consequently life has become a lot easier, even if people don't always accept "my heart tells me so" as a valid explanation for making decisions. However, it is widely known that even the toughest business decisions are made with the gut.

So, trust your gut feeling and allow your intuition to guide you to love. As one is connected to the Love, one can be happy alone or with a pet, friend or a lover. It doesn't matter if you don't have a chance to extend your love beyond yourself, what matters is that you can experience a real feeling of love. It is better that you do your best to find that tiny bit of real love towards yourself than expecting to be showered with love by someone else. Whatever your situation is, let this day be filled with beauty beyond all your dreams!

"My passion, both as psychiatrist and as Dice Man, has been to change human personality. Mine. Others'. Everyone's. To give to men a sense of freedom, exhilaration, joy. To restore to life the same shock of experience we have when bare toes first feel the earth at dawn and we see the sun split through the mountain trees like horizontal lightning; when a girl first lifts her lips to be kissed; when an idea suddenly springs full-blown into the mind, reorganizing in an instant the experience of a lifetime." - Luke Rhinehart in the Dice Man (p.12)

Rule nr 30: Purify your heart!

"Expand your definition, allow your conception of love to go beyond your emotional needs, and your whole perspective will change. You won't see failure and defeat. Far from it – you'll see the perfection. At every moment, from the second you were conceived in the womb, your life has been about love. Your existence is an expression of love, the only real expression it can have. Everything else is an illusion." – Deepak Chopra

Don't give more than oozes out of you naturally. If you don't like what you naturally emit, change your nature, and don't expect your nature to change in an instant. In the meantime, breathe in and breathe out. Concentrate your attention on your heart chakra and let its light shine upon yourself and others.

Ask yourself how can you make your soul to feel at home right now. If it cannot feel at home with the person you are with, take time to be alone and purify your heart by spending time with it, by giving attention to it. Let it experience everything it has to feel before you can let go of it all and start anew – with the same or a new person. Did you choose your partner because you soul chose him or her to fulfill your mission in life? For whatever reason you started the relationship, just remember what Carl Jung has said: *"Everything that irritates us about others can lead us to an understanding of ourselves."*

6th Meditation Practice:

Close your eyes. Pay attention to your breathing. Don't try to manipulate it in any way, just notice it. Now bring your attention to the center of your chest, your heart chakra. Notice your breathing again. Place your hands on your chest on top of each other, palms towards your body. Feel the warmth of your hands and the movement of your chest. Thank your heart for breathing and love yourself to bliss!

III VIRTUOUS ACTION (Love): Love Yourself to Bliss!

"I went to a bookstore and asked the saleswoman, "Where's the self-help section?" She said if she told me, it would defeat the purpose."
– Stephen Wright, Canadian comedian.

You ask and know with your thoughts but you receive by taking action. This part of the book is all about helping you to take virtuous action in order to receive the kind of life you have always dreamt of having.

If today was the last day of your life, how would you like to spend it? And if you knew you wouldn't fail, what would you do right now?

Rule nr 31: Open your heart!

"That is the miracle of love that we are completely lovable even when we are imperfect because we are whole." - Deepak Chopra

I am happy to notice that the years have actually matured me a bit. I have been able to increase the role of the Spirit in my life. Certainly my ego is still glad to receive positive attention but at the same time I feel like my soul is able to use the ego's happiness – positivity – for my spiritual growth. I asked for the fruit of the Spirit years ago and now I truly feel like I have truly been blessed by them. The fruit of the Spirit is a physical manifestation of a Christian's transformed life. Even if I learnt about them through Christian tradition, anybody from any set of beliefs can manifest them in him/herself.

The attributes of the fruit of the spirit are love, joy, peace, longsuffering (patience), gentleness (kindness), goodness, faith, meekness, and temperance (self-control). One can of course always develop further in these attributes or in the constancy of them in one's life, however, I think it was important for me to finally accept myself as I am – far from perfect but tentatively manifesting the traits I've been praying for. I finally feel like I only need to concentrate lovingly on my own development and let the other flowers bloom at their season.

My main mission in life as a human being is to get to know my own soul by increasing my awareness and capacity to love and be loved. How this will manifest itself in this life is a daily mystery that I'm grateful to experience to the fullest by embracing the little details of life. I can use virtues as a map but by connecting to my heart I will be guided by my intuition.

Therefore, in my opinion, daily practices of opening the heart chakra are vital. Instead of judging with your mind, just give it a try - no one has to know about it! One way to do this is to sit in a meditation position holding left hand on the heart and the right hand on top of the other and to be peacefully still, and perhaps you'll hear the symphony of the Spirit.

Rule nr 32: Manifest your dreams!

"In oneself lies the whole world, and if you know how to look and learn, the door is there and the key is in your hand."
– J. Krishnamurti

Everything that I have ever wished for has become reality if I have kept believing in it and really wanting it. I was able to rejoice for one fulfilled dream last week after a year of waiting and that made me think about the meaning of dreaming.

Time to wait is really quite irrelevant, what matters is the attitude and action while waiting. Life is really about sowing through dreaming and manifesting the dreams through meaningful activity, not so much about the reaping the dream harvest. Certainly reaping the harvest – witnessing the fulfillment of the dreams – is rewarding but the pleasure of the achievement of a goal lasts only for a while and then it is time to dream again so that through dreaming one is able to manifest the dreams through meaningful activity.

One of the biggest things that debilitates us from dreaming is fear. So easily I too become frightened of failure and very often my surroundings reinforce that fear in a form of a protective parent, well-meaning friend, or an acquaintance who tells about someone who really got burnt by life. Instead of trying to protect each other from possible failures, I believe in encouraging our loved ones to follow their dreams and let them know that we'll love them no matter what, and, if possible, help them through with our wisdom and know-how, but most of all with our loving presence.

I believe that it is not so much the failure we are afraid of but the actual feeling of disappointment and the conclusions we make from that. Like starting to question one's belief in one's capacity to live life in a meaningful way. People want to be able to want what is right for them and for others. They don't want to hurt others or get hurt, waste their or other people's time. I believe that when one does things out of love, one doesn't feel that time is wasted. What to do when one doesn't feel love anymore for the career they chose or for the partner they have shared their lives with?

I think that is the right time to ask the question: what would you do if you know you couldn't fail? Then time will reveal the right path. One might need patience or courage, or some other virtues to take right action. The right action is, first and foremost, to be honest and loving with yourself. Then it is to live your life according to your values and your mission (justice), and let others to pursue their life path (love). We will always get disappointed by ourselves and others, and that is why we need to be merciful. However, we will also need take a stand when it is required. One needs to be the captain of his/her ship.

According to the law of attraction, by being positive we attract the positive outcomes into our lives. Even if the law of attraction wouldn't work, the worst would come to worst and one wouldn't increase the positive outcomes, one would certainly have enjoyed the ride more by being courageously optimistic than fearful.

I am not saying that we shouldn't still listen and respect our fears, they have important messages for us to discover. But making decisions in order to avoid fear might not always be the best strategy.

Daring to dream means also not giving up on one's dreams when it seems like they are not going to manifest the way or the pace one imagined in the first place. Sometimes the outcome is even greater than one was able to hope for.

Rule nr 33: Take time to play!

"To live the life of an entertainer is living like a millionaire without having a million dollars." – Michael Ammar, Close Up Magician

We create our own lives through thoughts, actions, habits and character. As we've talked, first you have to learn to clear your mind of all clutter, for example, through becoming silent. Then you can choose what you want to think and afterwards those things will magically appear into your life. Sounds too easy? Well, it's not. It's simple, but very often the simplest of things, such as staying aware of our thoughts, are the hardest ones to execute.

What can help or hinder the magicianship of our lives, is our surroundings. Have we surrounded ourselves with people who encourage us to be free and creative or are we constantly facing restraints and complaints from the people who are supposed to love and care for us? This doesn't mean that we should just delete the negative people from our lives – that would be very unloving of us

– but we could try confronting the negativity by helping them to see the positive possibilities in our lives (after accepting them and their negative feelings as they are and giving them empathy for their negative feelings). Positive possibilities are endless, it is only our limited minds that create the false restraints. Therefore, we need more creative play in our lives to inspire our imagination.

In the end we are responsible for our own entertainment in life. Sure it helps if someone close to you is fun and cheerful but we should never expect anyone to keep us optimistic and make our dreams come true. Besides, it's much more fun to partake in making the magic than just enjoying its results.

How to have more creative play in our lives? By recognizing the rules to start with. A friend of mine asked me, why don't all of his dreams come true, and this is what I answered him:

I believe that people don't get what they want because (A) what they want is contradictory to another want they have, (B) what they think they want isn't what they really want at all the levels of their being, (C) they have to work harder/develop further/wait a bit longer to get what they want, (D) they are not willing to let go of what they want even if it would be better for the other people involved, (E) they have to change from wanting to imagining and living true their desired outcome.

Have you taken these "rules" into consideration in your creative play? What can you do next?

Rule nr 34: Love and be free!

"Your vision will become clear only when you look into your heart ...
Who looks outside, dreams.
Who looks inside, awakens." – Carl Jung

One day when three of my friends had their birthday, I wanted to give them something special that would make them feel like reality is better than their dreams. Anthony de Mello has said that we can be happy right now. We don't have to get anything or achieve anything to find happiness. We are joyful by nature. It is only the stamps that people put on themselves and others that cause us dissatisfaction. We have a natural desire only to love and to be free. It is of course very easy for me to grant these to my friends, so easy that it would be rather odd if I'd say to them that, as a birthday present, I grant them freedom to be free and to love.

However, when we talk about a romantic relationship, it becomes almost impossible to allow the other person to be fully free and to love freely. We tend to fabricate all kinds of expectations of communication and conduct – partly to protect the boundaries that make our own lives enjoyable and meaningful. Ownership seems to go hand in hand with romance because we are just following the golden rule: do to others as you would like them to do to you. We want to be in a unique role in our lover's life.

Certainly we want to be unique to our friends as well but we don't expect our friend to be a friend only for us, whereas we do – at least most of us – expect our partner to grant their amorous attention only to us. We all encounter trouble in our relationships due to these preconceived ideas. Getting upset will not, however, help anybody. One can only breathe in deeply and acknowledge the shared wisdom of all the mystics: all is well. Right here and right now all is well despite all of the discords in the harmony. What matters is that we continue to write the symphony.

Happy life is a continuous creative movement shared with others. We are to live in Love whether we have a romantic relationship in our lives or not because that is our natural state of being. We are to be the lover we want first and foremost to ourselves and then to others. I believe, therefore, that the best present I can give my friends is to continue to be present in their lives, to be a positive mirror to them; help them see themselves as objectively as possible, to remind them that all is well and encourage them to keep going forward in life – slowly enough to enjoy the scenery on the way.

Rule nr 35: Open your mind!

"Change is the only constant." – Lucretius

I promised to talk about the blocks that prevent people from living the joyful life and being in the flow. Last week I started in the flow but suddenly the next morning I had gotten out of it. Being aware and realizing that one isn't in the flow anymore is a good starting point. Then I began to think what is different to the previous blissful day: there was low pressure and I had woken up a couple of times in the middle of the night. The more significant thing was, I presume, the fact that I was expecting to continue in the flow. In other words, I had a preconceived idea that because I was joyful yesterday, I will feel joyful again today.

I decided to do something that has made me feel better in the past - and these things are different for everybody, which is why I encourage you to jot down what works for you. I did a bit of writing, yoga, meditation, visualization, had breakfast, and worked. Still feeling sluggish. Hmmm...

I decided to go for a walk – fresh air and a bit of exercise would surely cheer me up. Okay, I realized a few work related things I needed to do while walking and sat down to admire the beautiful sea scenery for a while. Then it occurred to me, I hadn't really been grateful about anything that day. I was just expecting things from myself. I expected myself to be enlightened enough that I wouldn't fall out of the flow anymore. Then I gave myself a permission to be a human being with humane flaws and desires.

I had seen *"Good Will Hunting"* – a great film on love – the previous night and watching it had created a subliminal clinging on to romantic love. Yes, I found myself out of the flow because I was too attached to my desire to be in loving arms instead of having the whole bed for myself. The desire was subliminal because it was clear to my mind that I didn't just want a pair of any arms around me but only the special ones.

This brings us to the core of the confusion of knowing ourselves: we are multifaceted beings with bodies, minds and souls. Our brains have four different compartments that tell us sometimes seemingly contradictory messages. Therefore, it is important to get to know all the aspects of oneself and work to bring them in harmony if we want to stay in the flow continuously. The inner harmony manifests itself as self-confidence, which is an important key to joyful living.

When we are in the flow, the only thing to do is to stay aware and let the flow lead the way. If we always add some margin to our lives and allow ourselves to meditate, we will always know when we are going off the flow. Then we should stop and let the natural course of affairs take us to the joyful flow that runs through the different seasons of our lives.

Rule nr 36: Tune your attitude!

"When you dance, your purpose is not to get to a certain place on the floor. It's to enjoy each step along the way." - Wayne Dyer

Enjoy the Steps

I love to dance and it has taught me many important lessons in life. When I'm dancing with a partner, I get the most out of a dance if I'm able to tap into the power of the present moment. If I try to guess what my partner is going to do, I'm not enjoying as much as I am when I fully let go and react to the music and body movements as it all happens. It helps to have the technique in place but the real art happens when one is able to enjoy the moment as something unique that cannot ever be reproduced.

Last week I reached two work-related objectives. It felt relaxing and made me more confident about fulfilling the rest of my dreams – when the time is right. We need to work in order to reach our goals but we should never get stuck in the "accomplishing mode". I keep repeating this to myself over and over because, for some reason, it is so easy to forget: life is here and now – it does not start when I reach an objective or fulfill a dream.

The attitude along the way is what matters the most. Are you relaxed, joyful and confident at this particular moment in time? If so, good for you! If not, why not? *"Who of you by worrying can add a single hour to his life?" (Matthew 6:27)*

Aiming at being "zen" whatever life deals for you, is the best gift you can give yourself. Of course you can also try to make the ride smooth by making life harmonious outwardly, however, you can never fully control the outer things. But you can learn to tame your mind, and when you do, the world becomes your oyster. *"He who has controlled his thoughts, is a veritable God on this earth." - Swami Sivananda*

Before you have your thoughts fully in your control, continue to have goals but, more importantly, do your best to enjoy every step you take towards them appreciating them as unique opportunities that you are allowed to enjoy only once.

The Free Gift of Life

I have this idea of myself that I want to be like: *"Love shone not from her face only, but from all her limbs, as if it were some liquid in which she had just been bathing."* – C.S. Lewis (The Great Divorce)

I want to be a perfect manifestation of divine love, and it is love that inspires me to develop towards my goal. I love the hormonal high of the infatuation that makes unselfish giving effortless. How could I, therefore, have a constant crush on myself and consequently be able to develop in true loving? Thinking what I am like when I have a crush and behaving accordingly – playing infatuation – is the key. As you play loving, you'll start to feel loving and that's when the change can happen.

My intention is therefore to make the *feeling* of loving a habit. It doesn't always happen automatically but it is possible. I always felt terrible when people said that they don't love their spouses anymore but they are still together because love is not about feelings but commitment to hard work. Yes, love is a commitment to work for love but I won't give up until I feel blissful every time I love someone.

Think about it, would you like somebody to love you back out of duty? I don't think so, at least not most of the time. As you want to give love freely, you also want to receive it freely. This doesn't necessarily mean you wouldn't ever feel too tired to love but then it is time to put some love into your own love bank first (or immediately after you have done the loving thing for another that needed doing).

The Universe, or God, or The Ultimate Principle on which this Universe functions (whichever you prefer calling it), works according the same logic. When you want something, you plant the seed in the Universe. Then you have to let go of the desire because only that way the Universe can give it to you as a free gift of love. Don't try to control life too much. Just learn to love and enjoy the gift of life!

I have realized that the best way to let go of any desire is to concentrate on the present moment, and the best way to concentrate on the present moment is to enjoy it. In order to enjoy it, I practice yoga or dance, read and write, dream with people I love or talk to interesting strangers with beautiful energies, go to concerts, watch a film cuddling in bed, cook a delicious dinner with care or go out to eat using all my senses, spend time out in the nature, just to mention a few ways I enjoy living this life. How do you enjoy life?

Rule nr 37: Practice virtues!

"Love is a condition in which the happiness of another person is essential to your own." - Robert Heinlein

Virtues for Romance

Virtues are the basis of romance. You need to cultivate faith, hope, love, patience, wisdom, justice, courage, temperance, humility and magnanimity if you desire to experience true love. You don't need to be the smartest, funniest, richest, and the best looking or the best lover to attract your soulmate. Our souls are always perfect, whereas our egos will never be. Authenticity and the purity of the heart are a great starting point to charm the right person. As one is authentically present, one can get in touch with one's soul, which is always lovable.

I have talked about the importance of virtues for an exceptionally happy relationship. Let's now concentrate on one virtue, patience, to dig deeper into their relation.

Children have a limited mind capacity that is growing rapidly all the time, however, parents need to help their children to make decisions when they are not yet capable of seeing the bigger picture. Parents want to give everything they can to their beloved children but they don't give them everything they want because some of the things children want are either not good for them or impossible to give.

I believe that our Creator behaves the same way with us. S/he loves us and wants us to have good time on Earth. Sometimes we mistake something to be good for us, whereas it isn't, and we are sad or even angry when we don't get the thing we would have wanted.

That is a call to let go. If that thing is indeed good for us, it will come to us. The same logic works with other human beings too with the exception of free will.

If you fall in love with someone and you think that you two would be a perfect match, you will get a chance to prove it one way or another to the object of your love. Then again, if you only think that somebody would be good for you, that relationship will not see daylight. It has to work both ways. However, if you genuinely fall in love with someone and you think you'd be the right partner for him/her too, all you need is virtues.

If you patiently and consistently show the object of your love that he or she is the one, the object of your love will respond. How else would you know if someone loves you, if he or she doesn't show it with time and affection? Love is magical and why we fall for someone instead of someone else is a mystery, whereas loving is very simple and straightforward, you only need to develop your virtues and serve the object of your love.

As I wrote this, I was in Bali and we were preparing for the change of year according to the Saka Calendar, which in 2012 was on the 22nd of March according to the Gregorian calendar. Saka is a lunar calendar, which was brought to Indonesia around 465 AD. To mark the New Saka Year, Balinese celebrate the Nyepi Day. Nyepi derives from the word 'sepi' meaning silence, hence it is called the day of silence. The main purpose of the ceremonies is to pray to God that He would clean the universe as well as the 'universe within'.

Nyepi Day is also meant to be a momentum to increase genuine solidarity and tolerance between people, accept the differences and similarities as a natural factor in life and put them in a balanced proportion so that together they can form a positive side of life.

On the Nyepi Day there are four mandatory religious prohibitions that should be followed by Hindu people in Bali: (1) no fire, (2) no work, (3) no entertainment and pleasure, (4) no traveling. These prohibitions help people to control their five earthly senses by mind and wisdom in order to increase the quality of life for the upcoming year. For people with higher spiritual ability or willingness to have higher spiritual life are expected to perform further prohibitions including fasting, not talking, meditating by focusing the mind on God and praying.

After the New Year's Day comes a day of forgiveness where people share happiness by visiting friends and relatives. The New Year is started by forgiving each other and forgetting the hate in the past year and working together to face the challenges of the coming year. Let's celebrate, then have a day of reflection, and after that joyfully and sincerely forgive all that has happened – let's give ourselves and others a real chance for a new, more beautiful, beginning – again and again!

Rule nr 38: Take life and love lightly!

"You can't plan in advance how to meet the next challenge." - Deepak Chopra

Ego Expectations

You don't want to be loved because of your ego – wealth, looks, wit and so forth. Therefore, why do *you* look at the ego of the other person? The world tells you to do so; very often people evaluate you according to your accomplishments and you mirror it in your own opinion of yourself and others. This, however, is not sustainable. The same way your soul mate doesn't need your ego to be perfect (you don't have to fulfill all the external qualities of his/her wish list) you shouldn't look at the egos of the people you meet.

It is actually quite strangely common that a person who has little to offer on ego level expects all from the other person's ego. I believe this comes down to the void inside the person. This person is actually trying to fill the void inside with an outwardly desirable partner. Let me tell you: this won't work in the long run! Deep down the insecurity would break the bliss, unless the person would somehow realize the need to fill the void from inside independently from the partner.

C.S. Lewis' novel *"The Great Divorce"* depicts a great example of this through the characters of angelic spirit Sarah Smith who resides in Heaven and the spirit of her husband the Dwarf-Ghost who has come from Hell with a busload of other souls to see their loved ones and to decide whether they could stay in Heaven or whether they'd like to return to Hell.

When Sarah meets the Dwarf-Ghost, his companion, a puppet called the Tragedian, starts to talk to her on behalf of the Ghost. The tragedian says that he has been worried about her being there without her husband and that she must miss him terribly. Sarah replies that it's not so, *"There are no miseries here."* Her happy response seems to hit the Tragedian heavily. The discussion continues and it becomes clear that when they were alive, Sarah had been emotionally weak and loved her husband because she needed to feel loved. She apologizes for not having loved him for his own sake. What upsets the Tragedian is Sarah saying that she is no longer weak and lonely, but happy and strong. He demands an explanation for why she does not feel pity towards him. She responds that she refuses to feel sorry for people that deliberately make themselves feel terrible, who use pity for a sort of blackmailing, *"hold joy up to ransom"*. The last words of the Tragedian are *"You do not love me." "I cannot love a lie,"* Sarah responds. *"I cannot love the thing which is not. I am in Love, and out of it I will not go."*

I've been talking a lot about soul mates but what about physical compatibility. Isn't it important? I believe it does play a role in choosing a mate even if priority is in the matching of two souls. Somehow it is easier for me to believe that souls are eternal whereas bodies aren't. Then again in Christianity there is a belief about resurrection bodies; when we die, we get healthy heavenly bodies that will enable us physicality also in Heaven. What about minds then? Are minds eternal? Some would say that we wouldn't need to use our minds in Heaven because there wouldn't be any problems to solve. But people like mind games such as chess even here on Earth, so why would we like to abandon our minds when we move on to another level of existence? Or does it all end after our brief time here on Earth?

I think that it is not so important to know what is going to happen. What is important is the fact that we live every moment of our lives virtuously fully anchored in the present. Why virtuously? Because that way we'd be prepared for Eternity in case it is true and because it makes the world a better place for us all. I also believe that only virtuous living is sustainable and yields everlasting joy.

As I've said before, the greatest virtue is love – the unconditional version of it. Love is when you love someone just because that person exists. Like any creator, who creates a piece of art or a human, loves the product of his/her creative labor. It is easy to love your "baby" because you made it, you expended a lot enjoyable effort into crafting your art. However, we should love everybody like that, like they were as worthy of our love as our own creations. There can be many things in people that we don't like – let alone love – still we should love them despite their flaws. This way we make this experience of life more joyful for all.

Flaws are actually an invitation to love. If we were flawless, we wouldn't need other people's love, yet we could still enjoy it. However, it would be harder for us to show love to a flawless person. How do you show your love to someone who doesn't need anything from you? With acts of service of course but does that flawless person need any service? What's worse, what if you are giving "the wrong kind of service" to him/her. Imperfections bring color into our lives. They are not matters of life and death. Let's take our and other people's flaws more lightly! Lets just laugh at the flaws, because they are actually quite ridiculous, and let's love the perfectly lovable people hidden under them. Then when you'll find a flaw in yourself you can forgive yourself easier having been merciful towards the imperfections in other people.

Love your mate with all his/her imperfections because the perfect soul-mind-body mate does not exist due to our inconsistent natures. Learn to love and let go and you'll increase the perfect soul-mind-body connection moments in your life. Just be diplomatically authentic because, at their best, authenticity is sexy and diplomacy is love.

The more connected one is with his or her soul, the easier it is to develop one's ego traits because one is not attached to them. The soulful person knows his or her own intrinsic value and doesn't need outer validation for it and is, therefore, free to love.

Playmate for Life

When intimacy comes along, I have to be willing to show my weaknesses and deal with the disappointment of my partner in finding out about my flaws and showing it in one way or another. I don't want to trouble anyone with my imperfections – I don't like the disharmonious chords in life's symphony. Yet when I'm connected to the Love within, I don't mind other peoples' imperfections at all; it only gives me a chance to show my love better. Seeing into someone with all the beauty and ugliness that is in there and accepting it all, makes love possible. Without intimacy there is only puppy love, but intimacy doesn't mean that you have to be serious, quite the opposite in fact. With a sense of humor that both individuals in a relationship can adopt, the couple can achieve real intimacy easily and pleasantly.

So, what is real love to me? Real romantic love is beauty and service, it is an overwhelming feeling of peace, lightness and passion. These are the qualities Deepak Chopra puts on soul's love in his book *"Reinventing the Body, Resurrecting the Soul"*: unselfish, giving, blissful, warm and safe, self-sufficient, needing no outside validation, innocent, uncomplicated, kind, compassionate, constant, expanding, comforting and sacred. I think that, in addition to fun, people have neglected the sacred aspect of love too much in our society. For example, we should treat our bodies like they were sacred temples. I believe God intended us to show love physically to only one person in practice even if in theory we should be able to love everybody that way. One of the reasons S/he wants us to have sex with one person only is because it makes life more simple, and simple life leads to happiness. If you have had sex with more than one person, it doesn't work the same way for you anymore, but it's never too late to start becoming more conscious of the sacred meaning of making love.

An important part of appreciating the sacredness of love is doing your best to really look at the object of your love with open eyes and listen attentively without any preconceived ideas about how that person should be like. I challenge you to grasp the complexity of God and human beings as they are without needing to change anything. Just look deep inside yourself and accept what you find - better, love what you find - and show it to someone who is willing to see into you.

I think that in general people should play much more. However, this should not be confused with being a "player" who manipulates people in order to get what he or she wants from other people. Adults should play similar games as children play. Unfortunately, I feel like the opposite is the case; if adults are playing any games, they are often highly damaging. I see the decadence of pure fun as a vicious cycle that goes something like this: women fall for players and dismiss the good guys. Then the players hurt the women who, in turn, become bitter. Each time it becomes harder for a woman to trust a guy and she becomes accustomed to live by herself. Then when a good guy approaches, the embittered woman is not impressed and doesn't encourage the good guy to continue to woo her and the good guy goes back to his nicely established single life and decides to forget women all together.

Players are smooth talkers and know what, when and how to do things. Women tend to neglect the good guys who can be a bit clumsy sometimes and can spoil the romantic mood by being themselves. But why can't women find the clumsiness cute? It is honest, genuine and, I would say, more interesting than the neatly packed players' advances. However, the players can be entertaining and I can see that, if a woman is under the influence of any mind altering substances, how easy it can be to fall for the tricks of a player and, if prolonged, mistake the manipulation of feelings for love. Love is an emotion that can be nurtured but it is not *only* an emotion. Healthy love makes sense and is joyful in an uncomplicated way. The excitement to healthy love comes from playing innocent games together - not playing dishonest games with someone.

Being a player in the negative sense of the word doesn't yield happiness to anyone. Even if the player can have a surge of enormously pleasing power through his games, the outcome is sad: the player plays alone. He is in control of the game but doesn't share the joy with anyone. I believe that the player starts to play the game after some painful experiences because he doesn't want to get hurt anymore. It's okay to learn to woo a woman but once you have been successful, let go of the power game and enjoy the joyful games two adults who respect each other can play.

Rule nr 39: Let go!

"You are right that spiritual evolution will affect all aspects of our life, including relationships. Sometimes that means the relationship deepens and expands into new areas, and sometimes it means a phase of development is finished and it is time to move forward independently. If a relationship ends because the two are not able to offer what the other needs to grow, then that means both are better off if they are free to pursue their next stage of growth. It is natural to feel some sadness and grieve the loss, but the love that was shared

should be acknowledged and appreciated as well. Even if a relationship does not last a lifetime, that does not mean the love it generated should be undervalued or diminished. It was perfect and right for the time and that is all you can ask of any relationship, whether it is for 50 days or 50 years." –Deepak Chopra

In Buddhist tradition there is a belief that all phenomena are impermanent by nature and this is why we should learn non-attachment. Everything changes every second – including our love relationships. Therefore, it is madness to hold on to something that existed yesterday, it would be fighting against our nature.

If we want to make a relationship last, we have to maintain the connection first and foremost to the Love within, which connects us to God or The Supreme Awareness, if you prefer calling it something more impersonal. Then that connection will tell us which way we need to develop. When we know that, we should communicate it lovingly to our partner. Then it is time for our partner to find out whether s/he can continue on the same path with us without compromising his/her integrity and spiritual evolution.

Looking to the past helps us to be grateful for the fulfilled wishes and to avoid the unskillful behavior that resulted in unwanted results. Looking to the future gives us hope and helps us to cope with sometimes seemingly stressful transition periods. However, life is here and now, and the past and the future should enable the full presence right now. Time flies by and the speed only seems to increase as the years pass. Don't waste it on indecision or jumping into conclusions. Use every moment wisely appreciating each one as a gift.

Be a blessing for someone. Learn to enjoy giving and you will be in constant euphoria because there are still lots of needs to be met in this world. Use love to inspire you to transform into the butterfly you were meant to be and help others to transform thanks to the butterflies your love plants into their stomachs. Don't let your love to become a prison, instead, make it a fortress for freedom that lovingly encourages transformation.

Compassion

Can love be harmful? Not compassion, the unconditional version of love, but romantic love can become an addiction just like alcohol or cigarettes. Addiction is the memory of pleasure, as Deepak Chopra has succinctly put it.

There is nothing wrong with pleasure or its memory, but if it starts to control you, it is really not a pleasure anymore. If you are in love with someone, you have to remember that you can never own anyone. You can only love someone and ask your love to be reciprocated. If the other person doesn't respond to your love, you have two options: to wait or to forget. Either way, you will also have to let go. If you can't let go of the result of waiting or forgetting, you could be addicted to it.

So, what to do when you have become addicted to love? One option is to deal with it is to write the chart of your romantic relationships. Becoming aware of yourself and the patterns of your love life may reveal something that you need to work on in order to live a more fulfilled life with more addiction-free love.

If man is a lover, he should be disappointed in love, because that is the only way to get deeper into the experience of love. In other words, in order to become a better lover, one should be disappointed in his ability to love. When disappointments in you or your partner come, don't get discouraged. It could be a sign that you are becoming better lovers. I think it is very important to remember this nowadays when it's so easy to meet people and start relationships. Sometimes you grow and move forward by meeting new people and having short relationships, and sometimes you are presented with another kind of possibility – a possibility for sharing a lifetime together. A relationship can end easily but it always has consequences.

Sometimes the disappointment in love comes in the form of being unable to receive love. For some people compassion can be so overwhelming that they cannot receive it because they feel they are losing control if they cannot "payback" the love that is given to them in abundance. I want to use the compassion I experience to pass it forward as best as I can, and not feel inadequate if I cannot, for a reason or another, show it the same way it was demonstrated to me. All of us might not be able to be compassionate with the person we have received the love from in other ways than wishing them well. Yet, we can always let the love flow to the outside world by paying the compassionate deeds forward in other ways so that we allow our lives to be abundant with love.

Can you bear compassion right now? If so, how can you spread it?

Seasons of Joy

Equanimity is the best way to react to whatever life throws at you; knowing that this too shall pass. Whether it is something positive or negative in your life, the lesson is to learn to let go and not be attached to it. The river keeps rolling on. There's no reason to try to resist the change, just embrace it by being fully immersed in the joy of the moment. Time flies and seasons change. Forget the decisions, just do what you can today to reach your dream or to keep it alive.

Don't forget that you also need to work for fulfilled dreams. So often people think that when they've reached a goal – be it a job, relationship, home, health, or whatever tickles their fancy – they should come up with a new goal. There is a point about keeping moving but there is also great beauty found in digging deeper. You can get more out of life by going deeper into the skill of a job, into deeper intimacy with your partner, keeping renovating your home, maintaining your health through preventative methods, and so forth.

Joy has many different faces. What does she look like to you today, in this particular season?

Rule nr 40: Keep taking baby steps!

"the Good of man is the active exercise of his soul's faculties in conformity with excellence or virtue, or if there be several human excellences or virtues, in conformity with the best and most perfect among them. Moreover, to be happy takes a complete lifetime."
– Aristotle

Life requires a little bit of effort but to me it seems that a human being naturally resists it. I want to be in a good shape physically because it makes me feel good and I'm able to function better – even mentally – that way. However, if the exercise hasn't become a routine for me, I, instead, choose to read a book at home. Reading a book is not a sin but will eventually make me feel weary if not coupled with healthy nutrition and exercise. This is why we should always strive to find the right balance of doing something we love and doing something that is good for us. The beauty of the matter is that the more we do what is good for us, the more we will learn to love the good.

That is the way to develop virtues – practice little by little. If you try to change your life radically, you'll soon abandon the pursuit and might even start to live in a more unhealthy way for a short while. This doesn't mean you should never do it. I think that pushing the limits every now and then is good too. Like Oscar Wilde says: *"Everything in moderation, including moderation."*

Don't sugarcoat your soul; you should not try to make life too easy for yourself. Easy life – a life that doesn't challenge you in any way – will not make you joyful unless you are fully enlightened. Try to challenge yourself and your surroundings gently so that you can feel proud of yourself at the end of each day, but never forget to be merciful to yourself and others.

Rule nr 41: Do it now!

"A garden requires patient labor and attention. Plants do not grow merely to satisfy ambitions or to fulfill good intentions. They thrive because someone expended effort on them." – Liberty Hyde Bailey

Don't think too much, just get on with it! Do what you know you ought to do right now. The longer you postpone it, the harder it becomes to do.

First, write down what you want in life. What is the myth or mission guiding your life? What is the metaphor or motto of your life? Write down the guiding words of your life somewhere you can see them regularly. For example my mission in life is to increase my awareness through and for love and my motto is to lighten up to be enlightened. So whenever I'm going to do something I do my best to check if it's in accordance with these two guiding principles of my life. Then if it is, I will do it without weighing too many pros and cons or otherwise wasting time planning the right time for executing the thing; *now* is the best time to do what we are supposed to do in this life.

On a more concrete level, you can divide things further to the things you simply must do like breathing, sleeping, eating, washing yourself and working. Then into things you love to do, things you might like to try and things that would be good to do but not necessary. Then start balancing them into action. When you act constructively, you are doing yourself a favor.

If you postpone something, you will easily begin to feel bad about yourself, and when you feel negative, you'll attract negative outcomes. Instead, love yourself knowing that you are acting as best as you can at this moment in your life. As long as you are acting out of the joy of action and for the benefit of the common good, you can be joyfully confident. Everything starts with baby steps, so be patient enough to stay aware of all the steps of your journey.

You can also reflect on the commitment of postponing the action. What scares about you in the action you are supposed to do? Can you ask help in doing it? Can someone teach you a skill that would be useful for taking action?

Rule nr 42: Take care of your resonance!

"Being at ease with the uncertainty and mysteriousness of life is one of the greatest gifts of wisdom." – Deepak Chopra

Life can change in an instant, even if it usually changes so slowly that we don't even notice it. Sometimes we love the sudden change, for example, when we meet someone who makes our hearts jump. At other times we are terrified, like when someone dear to us suddenly passes away.

I used to want to have everything as clear in my mind as possible and the idea of change was usually appalling to me because it would upset the harmonious status quo I had created in my mind and in my life.

I got frustrated so many times because of trying, for example, to figure out who to choose as my life partner until one day I realized it has to happen naturally like there's no need for choice because there is only one person I love and with whom I can breathe easily. This world is filled with beautiful egos and beautiful souls and sometimes they are even in the same package! So, how would you know with whom you should pursue a relationship, with whom to go on a date, with whom to be a friend and with whom a friendly stranger. I believe that you can know only with who you should be at this particular moment and if the next moment you come to same conclusion and so forth, you might have found the right life partner for you.

This kind of living and loving can feel tiring or it can feel exciting – most likely both. The main thing, however, is to take care of your own resonance. You cannot control outer things, and by trying to do so you only create misery. Instead, you should do everything in your power to stay connected to the Love within, to the source of all life and energy, to enjoy the joy. For me it happens through aware and balanced living where there is stability and room for change. We need to live consciously and true to our principles at all times. Anyway, what a privilege it would be to share a life with another human being dedicated to keeping himself in constant resonance with Love. When you are lead astray by earthly worries, someone would gently love you back to the divine sphere of the souls and vice versa.

Rule nr 43: Communicate with care!

"What is often referred to as love may be pleasurable and exciting for a while, but it is an addictive clinging, and an extremely needy condition that can turn into its opposite at the flick of a switch. Many 'love' relationships, after the initial euphoria has passed, actually oscillate between 'love' and hate, attraction and attack. Real love doesn't make you suffer. How could it?" – Eckhart Tolle

What Is Love?

Conflict and confusion in life often result from communication. We give different meanings to different words. I believe that communication has become even more complicated in today's world where we are in contact with people from all over the world speaking different languages as their mother tongue and associating the equivalent English words to varying meanings. Not to mention the difficulty of conversing through digital media deprived of all the cues of non-verbal communication – which in itself has national variations.

The author Stuart Lichtman gives a clear example of the complexity in reaching mutual understanding by asking us to describe the color green through association. We can actually recognize 1,000 shades of green, which means that your understanding of green is probably completely different from mine. This became clear as I, for the first time in my life, dyed my hair red this week. When people saw the result, for many it didn't match the image they had about red in the first place.

Colors are still quite simple and don't normally cause too much heartache, but what about words like "love"?

C.S. Lewis has written a book called *"The Four Loves"* in which he divides love into four different categories through their greek names: *storgy* meaning affection, *philea* meaning love between friends, *eros* meaning romantic love, and *agape* - the "love in the Christian sense" as he puts it. I think that as I have written about love, I have mainly written about the romantic love and the charity as C.S. Lewis calls agape intermittently.

So, when we are talking about other forms of love than agape, or compassion as Buddhists label it, I think there is always the possibility of getting hurt. But don't you think it's worth it?

Healthy Home

Have you ever had that feeling that you have found a place inside yourself where you feel at home? It can happen when you meet someone, or when you go to a city, it can be the work you do. At home you feel like you are easily understood and things run smoothly with effortless effort. Yet, the physical home for us is very often not like that. People tend to snap at each other. They only see things that the other members of the family have done "wrong". Why is it so that home is so easily turned into hell?

I believe the main reason for disruption at home is due to people taking home and family for granted. They think that at home they can be what they really are - even a very impolite and mean person. Yes, basically one can show his/her worst sides at home and still receive love in return. However, one should aim at making even a greater effort to be civil and loving at home. It doesn't mean one can never relax and let the steam out. At home one needs to have space to let go of the negative energy that has infiltrated one's being so that one can connect with one's loving soul again.

In the Nordic countries we have many saunas, where one can literally let the steam out. I see saunas as our meditation rooms. You go there to cleanse physically and mentally. Therefore, I suggest that the next time you feel like lashing out on someone, you go and prepare the sauna instead. Throw so much water into the stones that all your anger and worries melt away and come out of the sauna as a relaxed and recharged teddy bear.

If sauna doesn't work for you, go for a walk instead, or dance and sing while cleaning your home. The main thing is that you do something positive on your own. When you have raised your own spirits, you can establish healthy boundaries at home. If then one of the family members starts to play some control drama on you, you won't get sucked into it. Instead, you can observe it objectively and choose a loving and a rational way to react to it.

Rule nr 44: Lighten up!

"Don't take life so seriously, you're not going to get out of it alive anyway."

Lighten Up to Be Enlightened

One of my mottos is lighten up to be enlightened. I was once told that the degree of humor one can master reflects how spiritually advanced that person is. I decided to google my question for further knowledge: "Why is a sense of humor important for spiritual development?" Firstly, nothing interesting came up. Just clichés about how a healthy sense of humor is important for spiritual development and it is good to be able to laugh at oneself and so forth. Then I encountered an article by Ken Ewing called *"Spirituality and Humor."* In that article he mentioned an intriguing book: Henri Cormier's *"The Humor of Jesus."* I got excited right away and started to think that we'll have to explore this theme in more than just one blog update.

We just celebrated Easter Sunday and, therefore, I wanted to share with you Ewing's thoughts on Jesus' trial and resurrection: Jesus' *"sense of humor as it impacted His own spiritual life enabled Him to face with confidence His most trying days of passion before the Cross. ... There is an old saying that 'He who laughs last, laughs best.' And who had the largest and most robust last laugh in history? God, through the resurrected Jesus is able to laugh sin and death in the face – God prevailed not evil. It was God's triumphal loving laugh that makes it possible for us to have hope and humor in our lives."*

Being serious is simply not healthy, especially if the solemnity is accompanied by stress. Humor, which can help us to look at life from a healthier angle, is an essential quality in love. How do you, my dear reader, interpret this?

Getting Up Again

If you or someone close to you have acted in an unskillful way, see the beauty in it and forgive. Then confront yourself or the other person about it in a loving way. Behind our every action is a beautiful need that we are trying to fulfill. Get to that need instead of dwelling on the mess that has been made in trying to fulfill it.

I have not always behaved as skillfully as I could, and sometimes I become really upset with myself. I know, however, that getting upset will not help anybody. How to behave in a constructive and joyful way after one has screwed up? To start with, one has to understand what has exactly gone wrong. Sometimes it is just a vague feeling that things could have gone smoother. But after listening for a while to one's body, thoughts and feelings as objectively as possible – like as an outsider – one knows what is wrong.

When it is clear what has gone wrong, it is time to take action to repair the damage as much as possible and not to get deeper into the swamp. Finally one can breathe in deeply and acknowledge the shared wisdom of all the mystics: all is well. Things could be better but, hey, next time you'll know better!

The best present we have been given is this life of ours, and what we can do in return to show our appreciation for it, is of course, to live it to the best of our ability. As Eckhart Tolle shows us in his book "The Power of Now", in the present moment, problems do not exist and that we are already complete and perfect.

Rule nr 45: Be ready to receive!

"We need to give each other the space to grow, to be ourselves, to exercise our diversity. We need to give each other space so that we may both give and receive such beautiful things as ideas, openness, dignity, joy, healing, and inclusion." – Max de Pree

As I was writing this, I was struggling to figure out how to organize my life the best so that I can live my dream, until I realized that I don't have to change anything in my outer circumstances to do that; all I have to do is to embrace the fact that I have already everything I want. I just have to make myself ready to live the dream. In other words, I need to develop the virtues I need in order to live my dream.

Often we have a rosy idea of a life we want to live – including a certain kind of work and a partner, and as is was in my case a child that would make the dream life possible. Yet, it is just a fantasy impossible to fulfill because I couldn't live it true due to my flawed character.

Ever since I realized that I am not a victim of life but an active creator of it, I've understood that I'm the only block in the way of fulfilling my dreams. What makes life beautiful? I would say the combination of love and free will. We can use our free will to unite or to divide. Dream life, therefore, is formed through specific demonstrations of all kinds of love that creates unity among us. Knowing the core values and traits that I have and want to develop are enough to attract the right kind of activity and people in my life whenever the time is right.

Relationships are funny: we crave for them when we don't have one, and when we have one, too often we take them for granted and get bored or annoyed.

When I wrote this my situation was like this: I'm in a long-distance relationship with the love of my life. I'll be true to him no matter how he behaves right now. He needs to do what he needs to do now. I'm ready and I can wait because I'm busy bit by bit building my dream career. It's like he would be on a long business trip. One day the physical distance disappears and we are united. Not by a wedding ring or a house or some lawful agreements but by love that is impenetrable.

Rule nr 46: Allow abundance!

"Though I speak with the tongues of men and of angels, and have not money, I am become as a sounding brass, or a tinkling cymbal. And though I have the gift of prophecy, and understand all mysteries, and all knowledge; and though I have all faith, so that I could remove mountains, and have not money, I am nothing. And though I bestow all my goods to feed the poor, and though I give my body to be burned, and have not money, it profiteth me nothing. Money suffereth long, and is kind; money envieth not; money vaunteth not itself, is not puffed up, doth not behave unseemly, seeketh not her own, is not easily provoked, thinketh no evil; rejoiceth not in iniquity, but rejoiceth in the truth; beareth all things, believeth all things, hopeth all things, endureth all things... And now abideth faith, hope, money, these three; but the greatest of these is money." – I Corinthians XIII (adapted) in the Keep the Aspidistra Flying by George Orwell

Love and Money

The film "Wall Street: Money Never Sleeps" was a good reminder of the fact that even if anything is possible, we should always pursue our dreams in a wise and loving way.

I believe, that most people try to pursue their dreams in a wise and loving way but don't always succeed, and then they resort to unwise quick-fixes. Why is it that so often people get a somehow imbalanced relationship with money? I think it is because the people have, indeed, placed money on the most important place in their lives – like that sarcastic modification of the Bible verse from the Corinthians reveals. Fear (=money) has taken the place of love.

We seem to either struggle with our inner worth or we are too cocky thinking that we are more valuable than others.

This unawareness manifests itself in an ambiguous relationship with money. What complicates matters even more is that with money we can get many nice things that seem to make life easier and more enjoyable. I believe that abundance is our true nature, but holding on to it, is not. This still doesn't mean that you should be careless with money. You are not careless with your love or health, so why should you be that way with your money?

My way of looking at money is that, at the same time I'm working on increasing my material wealth, I'm also working on getting along with less. The real freedom comes from not needing anything material to be in a state of bliss – even if while being in human form it's pretty nice to enjoy all our senses – and according to my experience money helps in that. Eckhart Tolle has said, that those who have not found their true wealth, which is the radiant joy of Being and the deep, unshakable peace that comes with it, are beggars, even if they have great material wealth. So, I urge you to get your priorities right: be sensible but not fearful with money (remember that you can't take your material possessions with you when you die), love and enjoy virtuously all that the world has to offer.

"If you have 'needing money' in your vibration, then you will keep attracting needing money. You have to find a way of being happy NOW, feeling good NOW, and being in joy NOW, without the money, because those great feelings are how you will feel with the money. Money doesn't bring happiness – but happiness brings money." – Rhonda Byrne

Rule nr 47: Open yourself to love and beauty!

"God whispers to us in our pleasures, speaks in our conscience, but shouts in our pains: it is His megaphone to rouse a deaf world." - C.S. Lewis

Healing the Wounds of Love

Loving is worth it even if and when it will be followed by heartache. So what are we supposed to do when love makes us bleed?

When we experience pain, whether it is due to love or something else, we shouldn't try to push it aside or hide from it. We'd be better off concentrating on it fully as an objective observer and breathe in deeply. What makes pain more painful is that we let our minds make it into a bigger deal than it is. For example, if someone doesn't want to receive your love, it's their loss, isn't it? If you truly love, you just want to give. However, if you wanted something in return, it wasn't really pure love. You were using the object of your love to fulfill your needs. Can you then blame them if they didn't want to receive your "love" and ran away from you? If you truly love but your love is not reciprocated, it does not really matter since loving is a gift first and foremost to you – it feels like enlightenment,

100

provided there are no attachments or expectations involved.

The next time you feel pain remember that it is talking to you, trying to help you become more aware and truly joyful by getting rid of all the attachments and expectations. Understand why the wounds are there and they will soon be healed.

The Beautiful Surrender

Last week I wanted to be someone else. I felt like I wanted to be someone more talented and virtuous. I felt like I needed to develop my character but all I could do was just to stand still or go backwards. Thanks to my friends, however, I was able to feel lovable even with all my faults, and I smiled again. Yet, I still wanted to fall in love again but I knew I couldn't force it. The most beautiful things in life have to happen to us, we can't make them happen. We have to receive them as gifts. We can't earn love, but we can make ourselves more lovable by behaving like a person in love would behave.

And suddenly, after having heeded my own advice, I had the same enlightenment experience I had had a few years back after a major surrender, after I had let go of the idea of romantic love. The unity was amazing. Everything was so beautiful. The colors were richer and I felt pure, unconditional love towards everything and everyone.

This time I was able to analyze the experience better because I could now understand it also with my mind - at least to some extent. A pregnant friend of mine was with me when the enlightenment experience peaked. I felt like we were one and the same and I felt like I was as much pregnant as she was - she was just a different form experiencing the pregnancy. However, I could love the baby girl just like my own, just like I was able to love my friend like a baby - a pure soul deserving complete love, respect and nurturing. It was overwhelming. I didn't need anything. I was completely filled. I just wanted to share my love unconditionally and in a pure way with the whole world.

I had wanted to fall in love and I did, not to any man, but to myself and all the manifestations of myself that can be seen in every little detail of this world. It's indescribable really... And very inspiring. I'm now more and more determined to become my best self again so that I can love myself and the whole world better and more constantly.

Blissful Routine

I've been very happy lately but not blissful like I was blissful one afternoon in the end of June. I haven't missed that bliss but I hope that I could be in that state constantly or at least more often. To be honest, I hoped that I would have achieved that state by going to listen to His Holiness the Dalai Lama, but I suppose that for being influenced by his energies I was either listening to him too far away, or I was expecting it to happen - too attached to the result - and, therefore, not letting it happen.

I don't see any reason why I couldn't be in that state of enlightenment at all times though. It only made me bursting with love without any attachment. My goal in life now is to be in a state of bliss, not to achieve anything outer like a beautiful home or a flourishing career. I have been able to witness through reading my old diaries that the outer desires I have had, have all changed. I wanted a certain kind of career, and then another one. I wanted a certain kind of house, then I wanted another one. I wanted a certain kind of lover, and then another one. It is endless because we are supposed to play with those outer things while we are here on Earth. However, once you find the unchanging part inside yourself, which is the source of bliss and which unites you with the Creator and the whole world, you don't have to drift like a leaf in the wind anymore. You have accessed your inner anchor that allows you to serve the world in a state of bliss through your talents in a joyful way, and then all the outer pieces of the puzzle fall into their places effortlessly.

From connecting to this anchor, you will be able to keep the big picture in mind as you go on dividing your loving awareness to the relationships, work, home, leisure and possessions. I will personally strive to improve them all continually but slowly enough to keep it comfortable, yet at the same time constantly preparing myself to let go of them, to die every instant.

Happiness is in doing, not getting what you want. If you don't enjoy what you are doing, don't go changing your life situation right away but stay still and listen to your inner wisdom. Improve your health and self-discipline; create yourself a healthy and enjoyable routine that you can follow. Lasting bliss doesn't come from an outer source like going to listen to a guru but through a blissful routine that doesn't feel so blissful in the beginning but will yield sweetness when it is finally established. In the meantime, spend time with people who you love and who love you unconditionally. Get a breath of fresh air. Have faith. Be aware of all the little blessings you are showered with at all times.

Rule nr 48: Dissolve the Disappointment!

"Heaven on Earth is a choice you must make, not a place you must find." - Wayne Dyer

Pulse of Life

I began to think of ways in which we try to find euphoria in every day life. The Football World Cup started and there were lots of people with high hopes that their country would do well. Obviously, apart from the winning team, there would be more chance of experiencing lots of lows. Why then, do people put themselves through the almost inevitable disappointment just for a tiny chance of the exhilaration of victory?

It must be in our nature to strive for the highs in life. We feel more alive when we're high. Being alive, conscious in the moment, is the key to blissful life. Feeling low occasionally isn't as bad as to be in the middle all the time. When one doesn't feel the highs and lows, one stagnates into numbness. As one feels numb, one doesn't feel alive because there's no passion for anything.

Being able to face disappointment without resistance is actually an important factor in being able to live a peacefully joyful life. We get disappointed with everyone – including ourselves – at times in life because mistakes are an irrevocable part of life. Therefore, it is important to learn to deal with disappointments constructively.

Life is supposed to be lived passionately and therefore feeling alive is essential. One can feel alive without extraordinary things such as big sport events, but I guess it is sometimes easier to "resuscitate" oneself back to the pulse of life through an event that many people are directing their energies toward. I think we can find euphoria in everyday life by looking at it from a fresh angle. How do you find euphoria in every day living?

One practical thing I like to do is to thank for the coming day the first moment I wake up: "Thank You for this wonderful opportunity to experience this existence here on Earth today. I will do my best to honor this gift by being aware and embracing all the little details with an open mind and enthusiasm."

Breathing in the Pain

I think the most of our problems in this life result from either trying avoid pain, sugarcoat it or get a rid of it. The only constructive way to deal with pain is to accept it as it is and forgive the person who you think has caused the pain and acknowledge that this person is ultimately you. You have some sort of beliefs that say that if this or that happens, it is painful. Of course there exist "objective" physical pain as well but I believe most of it is psychological.

Deepak Chopra instructs that letting go of toxic emotions is the essence of learning how to forgive:

1. Taking responsibility for your emotion.
2. Witnessing the emotion.
3. Defining or labelling the emotion.
4. Expressing the emotion.
5. Sharing the emotion.
6. Releasing the emotion through ritual.
7. Celebrating the release and moving on.

In yoga there is a belief that if the energy flows freely in the seven chakras – energy centers – of our bodies, we won't get sick. We can help the energy centers to function better through massage, relaxation and breathing exercises. We can also aim to prevent pain by leading a healthy lifestyle, eating a balanced diet and getting enough sleep, but we can never fully prevent pain from entering our lives because we can never fully control other people's free wills and nature – neither do we usually control ourselves fully either.

Just acknowledge the pain for what it is, express it, share it and then release it. If you try to resist it, it will cause an energy blockage that will weaken you and make the pain even more painful. Pain is a mass of sensations, not a thing that is best experienced as it is and not to get caught up with thoughts about it. It keeps changing from one sensation to another. I hope one could face the pain with confidence ready to relinquish any resistance one may feel towards it through one's breathing.

Once the pain has been acknowledged, one can start becoming aware of all the pleasure that is going on in the present moment, like sunlight on one's face, the smell of freshly brewed coffee, the warmth of another human being and so forth. There is always something pleasurable in one's experience – no matter how subtle. If only one could let the pain be one of the things that one is aware at this particular moment in time, allowing all sensations to come into being and pass away moment by moment.

Rule nr 49: Be fully present!

"I think, therefore I exist" is the famous saying of Descartes and how true that is. But why on Earth would we be satisfied with just existing? I prefer to think that because I

love, therefore I live. I'll give you an example of how love makes us live through a story:

Once upon a time there was a little boy who had been playing with the finest toys in the world. He had been amused many times but after a while the amusement grew weary and he had to get a new toy or he would get very unruly. His parents were getting desperate, they didn't have any more money to buy any toys for him nor had they the time to make the toys for him because they had to work in order to put bread to the table.

One night before going to sleep the mother was praying on her knees to find a solution to their problem. She fell asleep in tears but woke up gently with the sun tickling her eyelashes. She knew right away what she needed to do with her son.

She told the boy that he has gotten sacks of new toys and the boy's eyes started to sparkle. "Where are they, mother?" the boy eagerly questioned. "They are hidden everywhere in this house, you find clues in your old toys, go and look for them." the mother urged her son with a calm smile on her face. The boy started to look for clues and started to see the old toys in new ways. Consequently he started playing happily with the old toys and forgot to look for the new ones. And they lived happily ever after.

Would you like to be someone who on paper looks successful or would you prefer being really happy? Being fully present with an open mind and heart is the key to genuine loving and living.

In order to achieve authentic happiness, I recommend you concentrate on improving the quality of your being rather than becoming someone who has everything that you now think a happy person would possess. How to do that? By learning to be present. Describing instead of interpreting is a good start. Then gradually let go of the description as well and just be aware until you melt into oneness.

107

Concentrate on goodness in you and work to bring it forth without suppressing your shadow side. I find art and sport as good ways to deal with our deconstructive side. We all have inner urges that tug at our sense of right and wrong, but if - through awareness - we are able to maintain them subservient to our moral codes of conduct, we will experience authentic happiness. With arts we can explore our urges in a safe environment, and with sport - together with right kind of rest and nutrition – we can change our biochemical balance and the urges become less compelling.

Rule nr 50: Just be!

"While I dance I cannot judge, I cannot hate, I cannot separate myself from life. I can only be joyful and whole. That is why I dance."
– Hans Bos

Dancing to Bliss

Dancing can be just a good sport; it's hard for me to motivate myself to run nowadays but very easy to dance for hours on end with good music. It can also offer a way of experiencing yoga: the union with oneself and the world through the unison with one's partner and the music.

There is no need for sexual connotations even if many non-dancers see it that way. It can be nice to be close to another human being just because it's also nice to be close to some other living thing – like an animal or a tree. I guess it comes down to sharing refreshing energies that the exercise stirs up.

I see couple dancing as a great way to step into the realm of the present moment because you are fully present in your body. It is a great discovery that happens through letting the music lead the leader while the follower can just enjoy the ride by relaxing fully to the unpredictability of the dance. Together with the music the couple creates a unique piece of art in the moment.

Of course all dancing can also stir up energies in the lowest chakras, but I suspect the stirring up has started already in your mind before you begin the dance. One can feel different energies and I just hope that people would go to dance in order to bathe in the thoughtless ocean of bliss, like children do.

Life is like a dance partner who never gets tired of dancing. A perfect dancer is someone who is fully present at the moment of dancing. He has a good enough technique so that he doesn't feel restricted in his movements. He is able to relax and play with the music. He knows how to listen to the body language of his partner and to enjoy his own movements. A perfect dance represents an ideal communication: both parties are authentic and want to understand each other and make it a beautiful experience for both. A perfect dancer makes you relax and inspires you to surprise even yourself. At best, something higher is dancing through the dancers and even the leader feels led. Just when you think it's time to rest after learning the steps impeccably, life introduces new possibilities and the dance continues.

Joseph Campbell has told a story in the *"Myths to Live By"* of an American delegate at an international conference on religion, trying to figure out what a Japanese Shinto religion was all about: *"'We've been now to a good many ceremonies and have seen quite a few of your shrines. But I don't get your ideology. I don't get your theology.' The Japanese paused as though in deep thought, and then slowly shook his head. 'I think we don't have ideology,' he said. 'We don't have theology. We dance.'"*

Walk the Talk

I believe I am walking the talk I've been giving you in this book; I am, indeed, enjoying the joy. It doesn't mean that I never feel negative emotions. I do. I feel sadness every now and then. I also feel hatred when something very dear is threatened. I do my best to stay aware so that I wouldn't dwell on the negative feelings. I just experience them and observe them and, if necessary, act on them. I don't mean that when I'm angry, I should go and punch somebody. What I mean is that the anger is telling me that something is wrong and I should do something about it – but never in an angry way.

It has truly been a joy and honor to dream with you. Manifesting dreams is not always easy. I haven't tried to give you easy answers and formulas to fulfill your dreams instantly. My intention has been to open your eyes to the little things in life that make all the difference as well as to open you to the idea that conflicts and paradoxes can be seen as a gateway deeper into the beautiful mystery of life.

Awareness, patience and individual effort are almost always required. However, the effort can be fun like it is for children when they learn for example to walk, and patience is required less and less if you enjoy the steps along the way to your goal.

I wish everyone a life filled with the simple joy of being!

Be You

The best help for staying in the state of joy is awareness. I've been guiding my own and your awareness to the things that I've found beneficial for maintaining a joyful state of being because it makes loving easier, but you have your own unique journey to discover.

I want to start my day by reminding me of my purpose here on Earth: to increase awareness through and for love. I suggest you do the same. Make it short so that whenever you are making a decision you can quickly check if it's in line with your mission.

When you connect to your soul/love/god within, you'll be able to feel a joyful peace that is beyond description. That is my wish for you.

I have lost my own joy many times because in general I'm a laidback pleaser who loves harmony. Because I'm very flexible in many ways and I've wanted to please everyone around me in order to live in harmony, I've lost track of myself many times. Therefore, my final advice is *Be You.*

Be you even if people will object at first when you don't comply with their requests. They – or the right people – will appreciate that in the end.

And *You* is a changing concept, so keep figuring you out everyday in a light way still remembering that you only live once.

"Yes, all of those swirling, pulsating energies of that which we call 'life' are welcome in the unlimited room that you are, the vast Living Room in which all of creation sings and dances and paints itself into the ever-changing picture of this extraordinary moment."

– Jeff Foster

Epilogue

Thank you for taking time to read my book. Did you remember to use the space in this book reserved for your own notes? Writing down your own thoughts and realizations help you to take your life seriously by keeping your heart light!

If you don't feel enlightened after reading this book a couple of times with an open and alert mind, and you have also done the exercises I have suggested, I suggest you'll read or listen the books by Andy Shaw. You clearly need to hear it from someone who uses a bit more aggressive energy in bringing forth the same message. I love his books *Creating and Using a Bug Free Mind* I received as a gift when I had written this book and I was editing it. They resonated with what I had written in my book and made me laugh due to the bold way they are written.

I keep re-listening to them because as he says, we need to keep retuning even after we have learnt it all once. Life forces us to wake up every day, to eat, drink, move, rest and go to sleep. Most of us need to do something that gives us money to have a place to sleep, as well as to buy food and drinks. In addition to that we need at least some social interaction.

Learn to enjoy playing your own instrument in harmony with others by tuning your movement to the rhythm of the Great Conductor that unites us all, and we can all enjoy a beautiful, never-ending symphony.

"Nobody can go back and start a new beginning, but anyone can start today and make a new ending." – Maria Robinson

The 50 Rules of Joy

I SELF- AND WORLD OBSERVATION (Faith): Dive Deep Within!
1. Know your paradise!
2. Be present and aware!
3. Challenge yourself gently!
4. Find your soul!
5. Love the roles people play!
6. Discover the real needs!
7. Experiment on yourself!
8. Be authentic!
9. Ask questions!
10. Know what works for you!
11. Remember the gratitude attitude!
12. See old things with new eyes!
13. Clarify your values!
14. Continue on your chosen path!
15. Picture your life!

II CONTEMPLATION AND MEDITATION (Certainty): Let the Magic Happen!
16. Seek Divine Wisdom and all the other things shall be given unto you as well!
17. Concentrate on something noble that resonates with you!
18. Clear your mind!
19. Understand your true nature through meditation!
20. Find sustainable energy through yoga and meditation!
21. Be silent and breathe!
22. Balance your life for health!
23. Know your boundaries!
24. Find out whether you prefer travelling alone or in company!

25. Enjoy the joy!
26. Keep hope and uncertainty in balance!
27. Meditate with art!
28. Meditate with quotes!
29. Meditate your intuition to fruition!
30. Purify your heart by giving attention to it!

III VIRTUOUS ACTION (Love): Love Yourself to Bliss!

31. Open your heart!
32. Manifest your dreams through meaningful activity!
33. Remember to take time to play!
34. Love and be free!
35. Open your mind and accept the flow of life!
36. Tune your attitude!
37. Practice virtues for greater quality of life and love!
38. Take life & love more lightly!
39. Learn to let go!
40. Keep taking baby steps!
41. Do it now!
42. Take care of your resonance!
43. Communicate with care!
44. Lighten up!
45. Make yourself ready to receive!
46. Open your hands to abundance!
47. Open yourself to love and beauty!
48. Dissolve the Disappointment!
49. Be fully present with open mind and heart!
50. Just be!

"The two rules for success are: 1. Never tell them everything you know." ;)

My Notes

_____

_____

_____

_____

_____

_____

_____

_____

_____

_____

_____

_____

_____

_____

_____

_____

_____

_____

_____

_____

_____

_____

_____

_____

_____

_____

_____

_____

_____

_____

_____

_____

_____

_____

_____

_____

_____

Also from the Author:

STEPS TO CONSTANT EUPHORIA

J.M. DAVIES

A customer review on Amazon:

"Apsara's Dance is a book about growing up as a person. It is a fictional story of a person who, through life experiences, learns to accept realities but doesn't give up her identity or dreams.

Apsara's Dance, though fictional, can be used as a guide for inner growth in life. The book title can be seen as a metaphor for a life journey. The writer encourages the reader to see life as a dance, trusting that life, as a dance partner, will carry you and lead you to the right place. In the dance of life one also has responsibilities: a dancer has to keep the rhythm, stay in balance, learn and follow the steps that have been agreed on.

The dancer has to also keep her mind focused. Maybe there is a more suitable dance partner somewhere else. Maybe there's more exciting music, a better orchestra, a shinier dance floor, higher heels... But while you are in the dance, you should not let your mind wander to things that are not there, or you might miss the whole joy of the dance.

The writer teaches that life's balance can be maintained with passion: I want to dance this dance and I want to do it with full commitment. Lots of dreams can come true when the passion is focused in the right direction, and there will always be more dreams to be achieved, but the writer teaches that one should not let them lead you to unhappiness with what you already have.

In Apsara's dance, the writer manages to capture the difficulty of balancing one's dreams in life. Every life is a tragedy, and every life is an amazing gift. How is one supposed to live it? Or is there any answer to that?

This guide book for life works perfectly as a fictional story because there cannot be a simple step-by-step guide. Why? Because nobody should be told how to live one's life. Otherwise it is not theirs anymore.

J.M. Davies' debut novel shows her sensitive and intelligent way of experiencing the mind and body as a perfectly harmonious combination. But her teaching does not end there. She points out through relations of the main character with others, that we are very much related to others: our loved ones, our duties, and the outside world as a whole. This book helped me to see that happiness is not all about me. It is about all of us. And happiness is not all about enjoyment. It is a mature, harmonious combination of realities, respect, balance, passion, thankfulness and joy.

I have never read a book, which can guide the reader so gently, without giving a single lecture or piece of advice. J.M. Davies has a true talent of changing people's lives in an effortless, relieving way. She does not preach but just smiles at the reader silently. But this does not mean that the book is full of sunshine. Quite the opposite.

I recommend this book to everyone, noticing that it can be interpreted in several ways. Read it as a fiction book with no deeper meaning, read it as a mirror to a young woman's heart, read it as a guide for more happiness in life for those of us who don't feel comfortable about self-help books. Or as a powerful novel of a life coach, who has a vision, passion and energy to make a dream life come true."

– Mirva Tuulia Viitanen-Kamal, MSc, Communications and Media Specialist

About J.M. Davies

After helping her clients realize their dreams as a motivational coach, Johanna Maria Davies, M.A., is now the writer and mother she always dreamt of becoming. Johanna writes books and articles as well as short stories and blogs in order to increase awareness through and for love. Johanna enjoys being present in her social circles and is grateful for the various sources of energy and inspiration such as dancing, reading, modelling and yoga. She loves to pamper her loved ones for example by giving them ReiKi treatments and cooking special meals. Nature is also very close to Johanna's heart and she does her best to live in harmony with it. Helping all the living beings to flourish brings her genuine joy.

Check J.M. Davies' Author Page to find out more:
http://www.amazon.com/author/jmdavies.

www.ingramcontent.com/pod-product-compliance
Lightning Source LLC
Chambersburg PA
CBHW070638030426
42337CB00020B/4062